Forged
ON THE FIELD

LETTERS FROM GLOBAL MISSION LEADERS

EXECUTIVE EDITOR
T.J. MacLeslie

peregrini press

Llantwit Major, Wales
2015

Forged on the Field: Letters from Global Mission Leaders

Copyright © 2015 Peregrini Press. All rights reserved.
Paperback print edition: ISBN 978-0-9933265-1-6

No part of this book shall be reproduced or transmitted in any form or by any means, electronic or mechanical, including photocopying, recording, or by any information retrieval system without written permission of the publisher – except for brief quotations for the purpose of news, review or scholarship.

Published by Peregrini Press, a division of Awen Collaborative Limited
For inquiries related to this book please email info@peregrinipress.com
Tel: +44 07597 170650

Scriptures taken from the Holy Bible, New International Version®, NIV®. Copyright © 1973, 1978, 1984, 2011 by Biblica, Inc.™ Used by permission of Zondervan. All rights reserved worldwide. www.zondervan.com The 'NIV' and 'New International Version' are trademarks registered in the United States Patent and Trademark Office by Biblica, Inc.™

Every effort has been made to make this book as complete and as accurate as possible, but no warranty of fitness is implied. The information is provided on an 'as is' basis. The author and the publisher shall have neither liability nor responsibility to any person or entity with respect to any loss or damages arising from the information contained in this book.

For those who have led
and those who will lead

"We are like dwarfs sitting on the shoulders of giants. We see more, and things that are more distant, than they did, not because our sight is superior or because we are taller than they, but because they raise us up, and by their great stature add to ours."

John of Salisbury

(1159)

Contents

Foreword ... ix
Preface ... xiii
Acknowledgements ... xv
How to Get the Most Out of This Book ... xvii

Week One

Day 1
Coffee break with Jim ... 3
Lunch with Fred ... 6

Day 2
Coffee break with Andrea ... 9
Lunch with John Love ... 11

Day 3
Coffee break with Robert ... 15
Lunch with Ash ... 17

Day 4
Coffee break with Brendan ... 21
Lunch with Sarah ... 24

Day 5
Coffee break with John ... 29
Lunch with Cathy ... 31

Day 6
Coffee break with Jo ... 35
Lunch with Roger ... 37

Day 7
Day of Reflection… ... 42

Week Two

Day 8
Coffee break with Faithful Jade and Morning Dew ... 45
Lunch with Todd ... 47

Day 9
Coffee break with Dave ... 53
Lunch with Christophe ... 56

Day 10	
Coffee break with Mel	61
Lunch with Dan	63
Day 11	
Coffee break with Ben	67
Lunch with Andres	69
Day 12	
Coffee break with Sandro	75
Lunch with Jeffrey	78
Day 13	
Coffee break with Linda Smith	83
Lunch with Todd	85
Day 14	
Day of Reflection…	91

Week Three

Day 15	
Coffee break with Tiffany	95
Lunch with Jim	98
Day 16	
Coffee break with Kevin	103
Lunch with Dave	105
Day 17	
Coffee break with Jim	109
Lunch with Keith	112
Day 18	
Coffee break with Theo Wilson	117
Lunch with Elliot	119
Day 19	
Coffee break with Jonathan	123
Lunch with Yung	125
Day 20	
Coffee break with Marcus	131
Lunch with Chris	133
Day 21	
Day of Reflection…	136

Week Four

Day 22
Coffee break with Taylor and Katarina — 139
Lunch with August — 141

Day 23
Coffee break with Mark — 145
Lunch with MYL — 147

Day 24
Coffee break with Francis — 151
Lunch with Willow — 153

Day 25
Coffee break with Jenn — 161
Lunch with Dave — 163

Day 26
Coffee break with Shad — 167
Lunch with Keane — 169

Day 27
Coffee break with Patrick — 173
Lunch with Kaylee — 176

Day 28
Day of Reflection… — 179

Week Five

Day 29
Coffee break with Yousef — 183
Lunch with Paul — 185

Day 30
Coffee break with Jack — 191
Lunch with Dan — 194

Day 31
Coffee break with Olau — 199
Lunch with Mike — 202

Day 32
Coffee break with Steve — 205
Lunch with Adam — 207

Day 33
Coffee break with Keith — 211
Lunch with Qua — 214

DAY 34	
Coffee break with Blaine	219
Lunch with Daisy	221
DAY 35	
Day of Reflection…	225

WEEK SIX

DAY 36	
Coffee break with Michael	229
Lunch with John	231
DAY 37	
Coffee break with JFK	235
Lunch with Tim	238
DAY 38	
Coffee break with Stephen	241
Lunch with Shane	243
DAY 39	
Coffee break with Mark	247
Lunch with Louis	249
DAY 40	
Coffee break with Hugo	253
Lunch with RC	255
DAY 41	
Coffee break with Kaldas	261
Lunch with Flavio	264
DAY 42	
Day of Reflection…	268

LEADERSHIP WISDOM

Afterword	269

Foreword

Recognizing good leadership isn't hard, but articulating how and why is. When bookstores were still a common destination, the section on business and leadership was filled with 'how to' books representing the latest recipe for success. As a younger leader, I spent hours perusing the shelves of Barnes & Noble while on furlough hoping to find the right approach. Then it hit me: There is no single approach or perfect style. Nothing that, when implemented, will cure the ills of my mission, church, or school. Leadership is as diverse as the people who practice it. If there is a common characteristic, it is probably influence. Leaders have it.

The question is how and why do leaders influence others? Initially, one is tempted to say that selecting the right leader is the critical variable. So we develop application processes, search committees, and interview schedules in hopes of finding the right person for the job. To be sure, certain positions require careful selection because the context and people are already set. Currently, I am chairing a search committee to find a dean of the school of theology. The primary tasks and qualifications necessary are clearly defined. If this search follows established patterns there will be dozens of interested people, but quickly the list will narrow to three or four people who truly fit the situation. In the end, we will ask which candidate has the strengths we absolutely need and the weaknesses we can adequately cover. Generally this is true of leadership positions in established organizations.

In contrast, leadership for mission teams, of whatever sort they may be, is much less defined. Situations range from a new team needing a leader who can boldly get things going, right through to the team that needs an empathic leader to bring peace and stability. These leaders need to embrace ambiguity and diversity over stability and clear goals. The boundaries are not well-defined and the tasks frequently lack traditional organizational logic. Thus, recruiting team leaders for a mission organization is a very different process than recruiting a dean. Qualities like stamina, flexibility, relational skills, and resilience win out over degrees or publications every time.

As a teacher of leaders, I will argue that it is important to study the subject of leadership to understand the how and why of leadership. However, when pushed I will equally argue that experience is without a doubt a great teacher! An effective way to learn is to reflect on your own experiences as well as those of others. That is why leaders are often keen on reading biographies. We have a chance to see how someone else handled the confusion of real life. They are especially helpful if the author includes both successes and failures. The reason is simple. We tend to learn more from failures than from success.

Nowhere is this more evident than in the Bible. The biblical narrative is a story of God's faithful dealing with his people over time. As the story unfolds it is consistently about God's faithfulness and grace, often through human suffering and rebellion. The story of God's people reinforces the need to learn from failure. Dependency on God is a mark of wisdom. That is why leaders who are worthy of following are often referred to as wounded healers or those who walk with a limp. One of my favorite images is that leaders should look like shepherds from the front and sheep from the back! Any way you approach it, we are followers of Jesus first. Leadership is a sacred trust that must be exercised with diligence.

Unlike the plethora of "how to" books that drew my attention in the bookstore aisles, *Forged on the Field* is a book about experience. In the style of letters to new leaders, the 42 selections provide a clear account of the ups and downs of leadership, leaning more heavily toward the tough lessons of reluctant leaders. As I read, the leadership insights captured me, often as though written from a shared script only because these godly leaders are clearly followers of Jesus first and foremost.

As noted by former CIM General Director, Oswald Sanders, Christian leadership is actually spiritual. That comes through clearly in this book. The writing styles vary from the more sermonic tones of the preachers to the self-revelatory of those who were surprised to be leaders. It is designed to help future leaders avoid the often-observed pitfalls so aptly recorded in these pages. It also underscores the value of the much-heralded strategy: multiplying opportunities multiplies leaders. Experience is, in fact, an important teacher. As this volume reveals, the global missionary movement is blessed with good leaders who are good learners.

As you read these special reflections I suggest you watch for the differences most often characterized by two major categories of team leaders: 1) western men, and 2) women and non-western men. The differences are at times subtle and other times transparent. As you read, remember you are reading the voices of saints of God who serve sacrificially. So, handle the differences with respect, yet with a deep sense that the reason for this volume is, in the words of Chuck Swindoll, 'to improve our serve.' Mission teams are multi-cultural not because it is mandated by their boards, but because Jesus commanded us to make disciples of all nations, forming a truly global Church!

Over the years, I watched as mission societies struggled to reflect a truly global missionary movement. Of course that was always the intent, but not often our experience. Please do not hear some sort of judgmental tone in my voice. It is rather a deep sense that we can do better, but with the absence of models we fall prey to reinventing the wheel …repeatedly. An international mission must have leaders in whom the members can see themselves. This list of team leaders is much more diverse than it would have been at any time in the past. Perhaps the next volume will be the two major groups of leaders writing letters to one another, hopefully with the same tender mercies and practical leadership lessons evidenced in the following pages.

I am thankful for this volume. Kudos to T.J. MacLeslie, the editorial committee, and the pilgrim leaders of Pioneers and other groups. May your tribe increase until Christ returns!

C. Douglas McConnell PhD
Provost and Senior Vice President
Professor of Leadership and Intercultural Studies
Fuller Theological Seminary
Pasadena, California

Preface

My son recently turned thirteen. As a way to mark this step in his journey toward manhood, I requested letters from significant men in his life. In the process, I was humbled, impressed, and informed by each submission. Each letter to my son was unique and personal, but somehow the combination became a whole. Although they were written for my son, each one was filled with wisdom and insight of value for any man at any age.

While preparing that book for my son, the embers for this book began to glow in my heart. I wondered what wisdom lay hidden in the hearts and heads of mission leaders around the world. We go through the fires of adversity and we are refined in the process. Our leadership is forged on the field. We learn valuable lessons, but unless those lessons are captured and shared, they remain only our own isolated experiences.

This project began in earnest as I wrote to leaders I respect, soliciting their input and their recommendations for other experienced mission team leaders. As the circle expanded and the letters began rolling in, I was consistently impressed. You hold in your hand a book of wisdom from leaders for leaders. In these men and women you will find companions for your leadership journey.

Let's not kid ourselves, leadership is lonely. Walter Wright, in his book Relational Leadership, warns of the inverse relationship between close friendships and the length of time in leadership. In other words, the longer you are a leader, the fewer close friendships you are likely to have …the lonelier the journey. This seems to be true for leaders in all walks of life.

Christian ministry leaders face additional barriers to friendship. People they lead often put them on a pedestal or otherwise create space between themselves and their leaders. Sometimes, leaders themselves unwisely feed the dangerous distance between leaders and followers. Over my 25 years of Christian ministry, I have had countless conversations with pastors and ministry leaders who feel isolated, many of whom were leading large congregations. The ironic experience of feeling alone in a crowd is a present realty for many Christian leaders. I have certainly felt this myself.

Mission leaders face even more potential isolation. Missionary teams reaching the unreached, or least-reached, peoples in our world often consist of tiny bands of people in far-flung locations. Mission leaders are often isolated geographically, linguistically, and culturally; all of this is added to their burden of leadership. Few people in the world understand their daily struggles. Few have walked a mile in their shoes.

This book was created by and for this last category of leaders. The authors you will meet and hear from are real-world mission team leaders. They have experienced the unique stresses and joys of leading groups of people serving the Lord in cross-cultural contexts. We hope you will find encouragement as you realise you are not alone. There are others who share your joys, sorrows, and challenges; others who wrestle with issues like yours. We hope you find wisdom here for your own journey of leadership.

As I have digested these letters, I have found myself pondering the wisdom they contain. These letters were penned with the idea of providing insight for new mission team leaders, but I believe even experienced team leaders will find them helpful; I certainly have.

May you be richly blessed by all you find in the pages that follow!

Soli Deo Gloria,
T.J. MacLeslie
Executive Editor

Acknowledgements

Creating this book was a beautiful process of drawing on the gifts and abilities of many people. I believe strongly in the reality of the multifaceted Body of Christ. Each one of us has unique gifts and abilities that, when united to the Head, enable us to make unique contributions to the Kingdom of God. When we are abiding in Him, following His lead, we will accomplish His will; but our contributions will be distinct, and flow from the gifts He has given us. The process of producing this book has revealed that truth anew. I gratefully acknowledge them here.

My friends, the contributors to this book, are the authors without whom there would be no book. They are my partners in the laboratory of field leadership. They are daily experimenting, hypothesizing, testing, and learning in the real world. If you learn anything in this book, it will be because they have done the hard work of discovery so that you may experience your moment of epiphany. Thank you, my friends and co-laborers. And to those whom have not had their letters and lessons included in this volume, please forgive me. Your lessons, too, were valuable, there is just not enough room to contain it all. Your work is not lost, it has found a home online, where I pray it may bless many!

Pioneers, my mission organization, has been totally supportive of me taking time to devote to this project. More than that, key leaders including Olau Thomassen, Eric Peters, Joanna Lima, Fred Dimado, and many others who cannot be named for security reasons, have provided support and encouragement throughout the process. I am grateful to be part of this band of sojourners!

Allen Hamlin was my early editor and a key collaborator throughout this process. He also introduced me to OneNote, which made the dance of collaboration more graceful and less like a mosh pit. Thank you, Allen for your work on this project, on top of everything else you have going on.

Neil Angove, my friend and the best book designer I know, has once again worked his magic to turn text into digital and physical art. Thank you Neil for your investment in this project. May it be just one more of many.

My wife and children have described my work on this book, particularly in the editing stages, as me 'being gone on a trip, even though I'm at home.' Thank you for your grace and patience with me. Sarah has also been a key partner throughout this project, providing perspective, and editing. But more than that, I am who I am largely because Sarah is in my life, she is the second best thing that ever happened to me.

The best thing that ever happened to me is still happening to me. The Father, Son, and Holy Spirit have been pursuing me all of my life. They have captured me, and continue to enrapture me. Though my heart is prone to wander, they never let me get far. Thank you.

How to Get the Most Out of This Book

It is difficult to imagine a more diverse group of people than the contributors to this book. These men and women from (and serving on) every continent except Antarctica stand united by one common characteristic: they are all cross-cultural Christian mission team leaders. We have drawn on mission leaders with decades of experience, and those who have only recently begun their leadership journey.

The lessons these letters contain have been learned the hard way, by trial and error in the real world. It is truly hard work to lead. And it is difficult to live and work cross-culturally. It is hard to try and fail. And even more difficult and brave to record your failures and let the world learn from them.

Each author has their own voice and has been shaped by unique experiences. Some of the letters are more general, while others have a particular category of leader in mind, for example an emerging leader, a young leader, or a new leader. Whether or not you fit neatly into the specific category they have in mind, there is much to be gleaned. While we, the editors, have made some minor grammatical and stylistic changes. As a UK based publisher, we have generally followed British rules for spelling and grammar, but you will find variety in style, grammar, and spelling as we have made every effort to retain the unique voice of each contribution.

This is not a book best devoured in one sitting. Take time to read and digest each letter on its own merits. With each letter, you have the opportunity to hear from these experienced leaders. As you read, you will find some letters clash with others. Practitioners in every field have conflicting theory and practice. This clash of ideas is to be expected. Part of leadership is to take input from a variety of sources, reflectively test everything, and hold onto the good.

It might help to imagine you're at a mission leadership conference. You are surrounded by hundreds of mission leaders from all over the world who are working in diverse contexts. There is no way you would have the time to grab even a few minutes with each person at the conference. Well, now you can.

We have structured the book around the rhythm of days and weeks. Each day you have two appointments: a coffee break appointment and a lunch appointment. We have categorized the letters according to length: The shorter ones we have called 'coffee breaks', while the longer ones we are calling 'lunch'. We are also including a day of reflection in each week, to help crystalize the insights you have gained. Over the course of the next six weeks you will meet 72 of our friends.

We would suggest you imaginatively seat yourself across the table from each author. Each letter will start with a brief bio, as I introduce you to my friend and then leave you to talk. You just received your order, and now you 'listen' as they share their insights and experiences in leadership. Let the unique message from each leader sink in. Read one letter at a time and reflect. What jumps out at you? What do you agree with? Did anything make you angry? Why? Did anything make you laugh? Why? What questions might you want to ask this leader?

We would also suggest that you use these letters for conversation and participation in a learning community. When we learn in community, we tend to sharpen each other, gaining deeper insights. We also tend to retain more of what we discuss. Perhaps you could select a letter for your team or small group to use as a foil for discussion.

We recognize that many readers may be serving in relative isolation; therefore, we have created an online space with a discussion forum. We would invite you to join in the conversation online. Click your way over to www.peregrinipress.com/Forged. Once there you will find a log in button at the bottom of the page. Click the login button and enter this code (Privateforum2015) in the space provided. That will provide access to the forum. In the forum, you will find space to discuss the contents of the book, as well as additional letters from other leaders. Some contributors suggested books or additional notes or references. In order to streamline the book before you, we have compiled these resources online as well.

One last comment to help provide some context for these letters: The majority of these letters (but not all) were submitted by missionaries with Pioneers. Pioneers is among the mission agencies with a unique commitment to team. The lessons learned by cross-cultural mission team leaders can be applied in any mission, leadership, and team context. That said, a brief explanation of the leadership roles in Pioneers might help to bring clarity to some of the letters.

Pioneers is team-centric, in that field decisions are made at the team level, but there are supportive leadership structures in place as well. Each team has a 'Team Leader'. Ideally, for every 4–7 teams there will be a field-based 'Area Leader' to support and encourage the team leaders. For every 4–7 area leaders there is a 'Regional Leader'. The regional leaders are supported by the 'International Director' and the director's office. It is not uncommon for leaders to transition in and out of these various roles.

This is a book by and for reflective mission practitioners.

We encourage you to chew the meat and spit out the bones.

Enjoy.

Week One

Week 1

Day 1

Coffee break with Jim

Jim Baumgardner moved from America to Bosnia & Herzegovina 16 years ago, became a team leader just a year later, and has served in various ministry and leadership roles there ever since.

Dear Leader,

Having been asked to share some thoughts and insights gleaned from my past 16 years of serving on mission teams, including various leadership roles for most of that time, here are a few things that stand out to me:

The first thing that comes to mind is all the classes and seminars I've attended and all the books I have read on the subject of leadership in the past 15 years. At the end of the day, very little of it has had a significant impact on me. Rather, what has impacted me the most was the personal coaching and friendship of more experienced peers, and older leaders taking the time to talk about leadership issues as they were happening…or watching as the issues unfolded. This was most relevant when it happened in the context of real life and delivered just in time; that is, when dealing with an issue, problem, or opportunity.

Many of us have inadequate understanding of what it means to be a mission team leader, based on where we came from: business environment, large North American church, or similar. I've found that for me the greatest help has come in the form of those who pointed me to and used the Scriptures to answer questions and deal with situations. One might think that could be assumed to be the first line of practice in mission team leadership, but I am surprised by how often it is not.

One leader aptly reminded me of the value of this verse and to strive to be this kind of leader who relies on the Word of God and whose faith is worthy of imitating: "Remember your leaders, who spoke the word of God to you. Consider the outcome of their way of life and imitate their faith" (Hebrews 13:7-8.)

I've learned that character and teachability are of greater value than skill and ability. Therefore, I look for those qualities in people and seek to live according to them as well. That means trusting that the skills can be learned and, if I'm out of my depth, then I can ask for help from God and others, while "striving always to keep my conscience clear before God and man" (Acts 24:16.) Being real and humble in a leadership role is also very attractive, I've learned; especially when it flows out of a simple but powerful confidence in how God views us in Christ Jesus.

Possibly the two most helpful leadership books I have read are Spiritual Leadership, by J. Oswald Sanders, and The Heart of a Servant Leader, by C. John Miller. The latter is merely his letters to those he led and shepherded. Very, very helpful to me.

Lastly, probably the biggest most important lesson I've learned and seek to pass on is that most people perhaps all people have a capacity to lead. But the character-shaping disciplines that go into moulding an effective, skillful, godly leader are best modelled, taught, and put into practice with appropriate assistance and accountability. Much of this I learned slowly after years of missteps and not being sure I was doing what was best. I could have learned these things sooner but mission fields and teams serving among the unreached don't usually have lots of extra resources or deep experience close at hand. I hope I can help others to be equipped to lead and shepherd sooner and more effectively, corresponding to whatever God-given capacity they have.

In closing, I note that I am still eager to learn in order to be effective and bear much fruit in the ministry of making disciples and planting churches so that God may be glorified. Moreover, I am even more eager to pass on the good I have learned and experienced so that younger men and woman may be even more fruitful and that their joy may be full.

Cordially in Christ,
Jim Baumgardner

Lunch with Fred

Fred A. Dimado, from Ghana, has been serving in various team and mission leadership roles for more than 16 years.

Dear New Leader,

It is such a joy to see you serve the way you do: running errands for the young and old, according much respect to everyone, the simplicity and humility that characterise your life; and even more importantly, your love for God and His Word and your devotion to prayer is very humbling and contagious. Do not abandon these qualities when you become a team leader, area leader, regional leader, mobilisation base director, or international director. These simple qualities are the very qualities that attract God's favour and which will carry you into His next phase of life and ministry for you.

In 2 Timothy 4:1-8, the Apostle Paul writes to his disciple Timothy, who at the time, was the pastor/team leader of the church in Ephesus. He charges him to preach the Word with "great patience and careful instruction." What a lesson on leadership! It is a far more serious thing than we have made it. It is about Him, His Word, His purpose, and not about us. It is definitely not an unending series of meetings and conferences to display our pitiful human knowledge; certainly not about manipulating power to serve our selfish ambitions. Leadership is about His will being done on earth and that leaves us with no option to do any guess work. "Preach My Word," He commands us! It is much easier to preach our titles and positions than preaching the Word. How will that look for you when you become a team leader?

In verse 5, he challenges Timothy to keep his "head in all situations …endure hardship …do the work of an evangelist" and to "discharge all the duties of (his) ministry." It is interesting that Apostle Paul knew that one could lose one's head easily when under pressure. Team leadership is obviously not insulated against divergent views from team members, diverse and sometimes unrealistic expectations, accusations, tensions and even insults and attacks from members. You will wish these things were not mentioned among believers in a team. We are so weak and fragile …and yet He still uses us in our frailty as missional agents for His glory. Brother, may the grace of God be sufficient for all of us to keep our heads in all situations!

One major lesson that I have learnt and experienced is the fact that enduring hardship for the Lord is a major wheel upon which mission thrives. Money has a significant role to play in missions but I daresay that the most compelling testimonies – and where the Lord is clearly working – are in places where people are simply pressing on in faith through hardship and great sacrifice. The Apostle Paul had endured hardship several times: beaten, stoned, left for dead, shipwrecked, imprisoned, and isolated. How may a challenge of enduring hardship impact on you when become a team leader?

I grew up in a tribe where pouring drink offerings to the gods as a sacrifice was a common and constant phenomenon around me. The fetish priests and priestesses knew that pouring libation was an act of consecration and sacrifice. They knew that something needed to be given up for a certain goal to be realised. The Apostle Paul writes in v.6 that he was "being poured out like a drink offering," a symbol of consecration and sacrifice. From his life we glean lessons on leadership regarding consecration, holiness, and character; and about emptying ourselves into others for the Lord's use and glory. A few years ago, I served directly under Dr. Solomon Aryeetey, base director of Pioneers Africa at the time. He would craft difficult e-mails and ask me to read them and give him feedback. A number of the e-mails were quite punchy and difficult to read. Sometimes I mustered courage to say, "Uncle Solo, this one is not good." He was most times gracious and would immediately delete an eight-page mail and start all over again after a week or two. The second attempt was always beautiful. Little did I know then, that Dr. Aryeetey was pouring his life into mine even by teaching me the art and science of crafting e-mails which glorify the Lord and honour the recipient as well. Leadership is not about living in a closet, shrouded in mystery; it has to be an open, transparent life, constantly poured out into the lives of those we are called to serve …and for the Lord's glory.

My dear sibling in the Lord, thank you for allowing me to share these thoughts and experiences with you. You have in many ways poured your life into others even though you may not yet consider yourself as a leader. Thank you!

May the Lord help us to preach the Word, to keep our heads in all situations, to endure hardship, and to pour our lives out like a drink offering for His glory alone.

Your brother,
Fred Dimado

Week 1

Day 2

Coffee break with Andrea

Andrea Dorigo and his wife McKenzie have been serving for the last six years in his home country of Italy. Although they have desired to build a team for years, only recently have they received co-workers.

Dear Leader,

Here are a few thoughts I'd like to share with you as you step into a team leadership role:

Being a multicultural team leader has been a challenging role. We are working in Italy and I'm Italian. On our team we have Italians, Americans, and Australians. Initially I thought that my role was helping them to get settled and start to understand and adapt to the new Italian culture; but after much time I have realised that for me to help them understand and adapt to my/the local culture I personally had to start discovering their culture – where they were coming from – and not discard it.

Lots of times when new team members come they say they don't have many expectations for the first couple of years while they are in language and culture learning; but I have realised that that is just a myth. Everyone comes with big expectations of what it is going to be, like being able to learn the language in a few months …when most likely it will take a year or more.

What I was able to realise was that I too had big expectations of them. I was expecting them to act in the way I had planned it in my mind. When both my and their expectations shattered, we found it really challenging to figure out how to put all the pieces together.

What this is teaching me is that it is very important, when a new team is starting or when new teammates arrive, to remember that not everyone understands everything of how things work. And it is really important in the beginning stages to take time to get to know each other, understand where we come from, talk through past experiences that maybe can help us move forward, and mostly to have grace for one another.

During the two years of culture and learning language of my teammates, one of my mistakes was not protecting their language learning time enough. Because of our particular situation I sometimes let them get involved into many ministry things that they maybe didn't understand yet, and which stressed them out, making them lose attention on culture and language learning.

At the present time, we have had to refocus, encourage and emphasise the importance of involving themselves only in things that are beneficial to their language and culture learning process. My wife and I had to be careful to not involve them in conversations and ministry things that can be a distracting and stressful for them. It is hard at times because my wife and I have been working here for the last six years without team, and now for the first time we are excited to do ministry together with a team. But it is really tricky, because we are in a completely different stage than they are and it is difficult to find a balance.

All of this is a lot of practical things, but the most important is that we remember that we need to keep our eyes on Jesus and not on ourselves. We are His tools and He knows best how to use them. When we take our eyes off of Him we start losing direction, and we try to get things done in our own way and in our own strength. In the midst of team trouble, Jesus is our anchor; and also with differences we can find oneness in Him.

Hope this helps. God Bless,
Andrea

Week 1 : Day 2 :

Lunch with John Love

John Love Fain left South Carolina three decades ago and began his mission career in the islands of South East Asia. Not long after his arrival on the field, he was called upon to take up a team leadership role. In the years since, John Love has served in many team, field, and organizational leadership roles.

Dear Leader,

Although I may not know you, I hope you don't mind if I take some liberties in sharing my heart with you on the crying need of the hour: God-exalting leadership. We find ourselves in perilous times and we desperately need people who will lead those entrusted into their care into a new tomorrow. I believe God wants to use each of us in this way so that the Lord Jesus Christ will be extravagantly adored among the nations and in each one of our lives.

What kind of leaders are needed in our day?

We need those who will fear nothing but sin, devoting themselves without hesitation to knowing Him and obeying all He has revealed to us. More than anything else, we need leaders who will unashamedly love God more than life or death, reputation or fame, far above all other earthly affections.

This requires us to grapple daily with the idolatry of our own hearts and the wonder of a perfect Savior offering us a transforming Gospel. Let the beauty and symmetry of His holiness bring you daily face-down before Him. From that posture of utter humility, let Him guide you through every decision and relationship.

As leaders, Jesus calls us to an impossible love, one that sees others from His Father's heart. Allow the riches of His grace and incomparably great power to give you what is needed to love well your family, your colleagues, and the unreached. Empty yourself and become the servant

He has called you to be, and history itself will be rewritten. Nothing can stand against God's unconquerable love.

Let no one and nothing in this world draw you away from the beauty of His Word. Eat the Book. Don't let it depart from your mouth. Meditate on it day and night. Let God's Word, not people's interpretation of it, guide you as you seek Him in community with your family and those you serve. Find your deepest satisfaction in the Word as it points you to the Living Word. Drink lustily from these cool, soul-satisfying waters. Let integrity in all things pertaining to life and godliness be defined as coming underneath these ancient truths.

Show others what it means to walk in freedom and victory. Let no one and no problem snatch away the full measure of His joy offered to you. Lead others to the Living Waters where they too will find "life more abundant." Let Him orchestrate your lives however He desires, knowing that pain, discouragement, disillusionment, and despair are the building blocks to full surrender and unparalleled freedom! Embrace all of life for the precious gift that it is, and help others to do the same. Never settle for less than His best in any matter, even when persecution, misunderstanding, or heartache may result. That is leadership which pleases Him!

Forgive even as Christ has forgiven you. Perhaps the most radical and transformative leadership is modelling what it is to forgive from the heart completely and permanently. Do so courageously and without looking back. May it be impossible to explain your life and leadership outside of the Person of Christ! Pray God will strengthen and empower you to love others daily, maturely, selflessly, and without hesitation even as He has loved us.

There are many practical implications which flow from this servant-leadership, God-centered framework. Here are just a few:

Never compare yourself with others. Be comfortable in your own skin knowing He has a unique contribution for your life which only you can make.

Hold all leadership roles with an open hand. Never allow your sense of identity to be defined by a leadership position. All that matters when we stand before Him will be whether or not we faithfully accomplished what was asked of us, and whether or not we attempted to do so in His power, not our own. Period.

Understand that life will always be hard. We will never develop in our leadership to the point where we have arrived. You will find deeper mysteries, more profound desperation, and ever greater challenges the older you get. Learn to laugh at these realities knowing that He who called you is faithful and most certainly He will do it! He will never leave us or forsake us. Therefore, we can trust Him no matter how dark the night or confusing our experience! That truth makes every relationship, the most mundane responsibilities, and all our painful disappointments of eternal value! This transcends all aspects of our leadership calling.

In closing, remember that we have already died (Colossians 3.) Therefore, as His called-out leaders we set our hearts on things above where Christ is seated at the right hand of God. We set our minds on things above and not on earthly things. Make it your mission to help all those under your care to do just that! As we do so, His glory will be seen and honored in this fallen generation. Heaven will be populated with God-lovers. The most unlikely of people from every generation will someday bow with us before His throne. The glories of His character will be revealed in breathless wonder! What could be greater than that?!

Yes… leadership matters.

Your fellow worshipper,
John Love

Week 1
Day 3

Coffee break with Robert

Born and raised in Sub-Saharan Africa, Robert Smith has spent the last 10 years serving among the unreached in the United Kingdom and the last eight as a team leader.

Dear Team Leader,

So you have a vision? Even if you know the destination, you're unlikely to know the exact path. But there is One who does! My advice is to stay close to Him. Turn neither to the right nor to the left without His say-so. You can do no better than to follow Jesus' example – and He only did what His Father said. So resolve now to jealously guard your daily times of communion with God. Make that your number one priority! You don't need to get formulaic or legalistic about it – just make sure you spend time with Him. Figure out the ways that most easily bring you into His Presence and enable you to hear from Him. Set in place systems that will reveal when you are drifting away from Him. Never rely on your own wisdom, your own experience, your own ability, or your own apparent success – rely only on Him! Don't be distracted by the demands or approval of this world – look only to Him!

Don't fool yourself into thinking you are all alone or that you can do this all on your own. You need others and others need you. This requires humility. Learn from those who have gone before you. Acknowledge those whom God has called to work alongside you – your spouse, your children, your teammates, your co-workers, your fellow brothers and sisters in the Church, and maybe even some non-believers. Make serving them part of your vision.

Lead your team with integrity. Don't fall into the trap of pretending to be someone you are not. You may lose face – but so what? The more open you are with your team, the more they will be able to support you and the more open they will be with you in return. Allow them to be themselves – who God truly made them to be. Use whatever tools are available to enable them to discover their strengths and weaknesses. Celebrate one another's strengths and allow much grace for the weaknesses.

For His Glory,
Robert

Week 1: Day 3:

Lunch with Ash

Ash Seaton, from Australia, served for 10 years in South East Asia and lead a CP team for eight years amongst a Hindu unreached people group. The team is still working together there, while Ash has recently moved into a field leadership role.

Dear Friend,

I wanted to write a brief note of reflection, remembering the things I believe the Lord has taught me through this journey of leading a cross-cultural church planting team. For me, the team leadership journey was a tremendous privilege, a journey of great joys mixed in with challenges like I had never faced before. Throughout everything, it was our team that kept my family going through difficult times; and it is our team that is still a great source of celebration and joy, a discipleship community of whom I am continually thankful!

So, what would I pass on? What would I challenge you to consider? The three things that stand out are primarily works that God did in my own heart. I wonder if they are healthy lessons for us all.

Firstly, always listen to God! This team is not yours; it is His. As you walk this journey, remember that God is at work – He always is – and has been amongst these unreached people well before you and your team came along. He has called you to serve: to serve Him and to serve your team.

Both of these require a daily posture of listening to God and asking, "What are you doing Lord?" and, "How is it, Lord, that you want this team to work with You?" Please don't be naïve like I often was, in thinking that because you are called the leader, you know what is best for the team. Only God really knows what is best, and only through a complete listening surrender to Him, holding your team before Him with an open hand, will you be able to serve both Him and your team well. Remember, to serve this team as their leader is a gift, it is not a right. God may ask you to give it up; be ready to listen!

Secondly, this community that we call team is a discipleship community; be careful to take the posture of a disciple within this community.

Yes, you need to lead and you need to present vision with clarity; but, first and foremost, you are a disciple of Jesus. As the leader, you must also model what it means to follow well. Part of the journey of discipleship is the important role of the body of Christ (your team) to sharpen, rebuke, and spur us on in our walk with Jesus. Be a learner and a disciple as you embrace the tremendous value of fellow brothers and sisters in team who also are listening to God and seeking to follow after Him. As you follow Jesus well, God will empower you to lead His disciples well. There will be many weaknesses in your own life and in the lives of your teammates, much of which you don't yet realise. This, however, is the power of living in a discipleship community like your team! Don't hesitate to embrace the refining process of being in community with fellow disciples; embrace it and model for your team what it looks like to walk this refining process together. This discipleship community is a powerful witness to the unreached people you are amongst, so, lead as a disciple of Jesus!

Lastly, continually search for ways to encourage the heart and celebrate the successes of your team. Spend a lot of time learning about those you lead. Understand their passions, their gifts, their weaknesses, and work hard to find creative ways to empower them in roles that are consistent with who God made them to be. Encouragement is so important, even if it doesn't come naturally for you. Routinely seek out ways that you can specifically and publically recognise and encourage the value of each team member. This will build trust and commitment within, and to, your discipleship community. Life in a cross-cultural setting can be extremely difficult; your team needs to hear you affirming and valuing their presence and contribution. The enemy will be feeding them many lies throughout this process.

Also, develop a culture of celebration, both at the individual level and corporately. Be sure to help your team to set good strategic goals and always celebrate successfully completing those goals; it encourages the heart. God is always working around us, both in ways that are obvious to us and also in the sometimes more subtle things. God will be drawing people to Himself, He will be constantly doing a refining work in your own lives, so be careful to be thankful for all that is happening in the spiritual realms; it encourages the heart. Teach your team to frequently recognize what God is doing in your lives and through your team, and give Him praise! Celebrate success!

May the Lord bless you in this pilgrimage that we call team leadership.

A disciple of Jesus,
Ash

Week 1
Day 4

Coffee break with Brendan

Brendan Meyerink and his family moved from Australia to the Republic of Ireland five years ago, where they started a team in partnership with local churches to see more churches established.

Dear Leader,

Thanks for the invitation to share some lessons learnt from my leadership experience with you.

When I think about leadership I simultaneously get excited and also grimace under the burden of responsibility. To be honest, being a leader is something I both love and hate, like the *Divinyls'* song goes, "It's a fine line between pleasure and pain!"

As I began in leadership I was full of admiration for the heroic and cutting-edge style leader who would bravely take a team enamoured with great vision into unchartered waters on daring adventures. Instead, what I now admire and appreciate is that leadership is more about staying behind the ship's wheel, keeping your ministry pointing into the waves, and avoiding getting broadside to the swell and capsizing. It sounds like a bleak and depressing outlook on ministry leadership, but it has been a reality for me that much of the time it's a battle to feel like you're going anywhere at all. The measure of success has been being able maintain the course even if the going is slow. So my heroes in leadership now are those who have endured in leadership, who have waded and continue to wade through boggy ground but retain their passion for the Lord and for ministry.

When I first began in leadership, I was naturally untried and therefore idealistic. The greatest challenge to my idealism has been disappointments – none greater than disappointing myself through not being able to achieve expectations I had set both for ministry and myself. My disappointments have led me to a new perspective, which has humbled me, loosened my grip on leadership, and allowed me to surrender it to God. It becomes easier over time to surrender it to God because it brings freedom which releases the burdens that I hate carrying. It feels better to be freer, and I can see myself persevering in ministry when I'm not feeling like I need to drag myself and others forward.

Strangely, as I continue as a leader, it is the things I have hated doing that have become for me the most stimulating because they are where the greatest growth and change has been, both for me and for others! The fun stuff is great because you can often pick and choose what you want to do or not. The grimacing stuff is mostly the stuff you have no choice other than to plough through it, usually with great difficulty. My areas of greatest pride in my leadership have been the things I have found on the other side of adversity or struggle; I value them more.

One of the mistakes I have made in my leadership was to value relationships with the community more than relationships within my mission team. As an evangelist my focus was on making connections with the community that I had moved into. I put much more value on those friendships and prioritised them more than my relationship with teammates. Although I am now aware of this and I dearly love my teammates, I need to consciously work at spending personal time with my team and making sure there is genuine love, friendship, and support there. This is an area where I acknowledge I need to grow more.

An important lesson I have learnt in my leadership is that it's ok to have my weaknesses and have others know about them. The image of a leader that has it all together and shows no cracks is one that no one really wants to follow. I have found that sharing honestly about the struggles, weaknesses, blind spots, and insecurities with my team has led to stronger relationships and trust. As I have 'bared all' to my team, they have been more open with myself and others in return.

May God grow you, shape you, and work through you in your leadership.

Brendan

Lunch with Sarah

*S*arah Joseph ministered full-time for 10 years in America, before embarking for East Asia where she has spent the last 10 years serving in various roles, including two years as a team leader.

Dear New Team Leader,

There have been volumes upon volumes written about the subject of leadership. I would never consider myself an expert on the subject, and anything that I would write about leadership has most likely already been written before. The one thing, however, that I can share with you is my own experience. As I reflect on almost 20 years of Christian ministry, there are a few truths that I have gleaned over the years that I wish I had known when I first began this journey so many years ago. I think knowing these truths would have made me a better leader, and it also would have helped me understand some of my own frustrations with certain team situations. I share my perspective as someone who has served under various leaders and also as someone who has served as a leader. I hope they might help you as you reflect on the journey that lies ahead of you!

Leadership is not a position. Of course a position gives you authority and a platform, but it is not what ultimately makes you a leader. I would argue that true leadership is following Christ in love and obedience and encouraging others to do the same. It is asking others to come along with you as you walk with the Lord (1 Peter 5:3.) We have all known people in positions of authority that no one wants to follow; and conversely we have all known people who hold no formal position but exert a tremendous amount of influence simply by how they conduct their lives. How are you living your life? Are you the kind of person people actually want to follow? How is your walk with the Lord? Let your walk with the Lord be the foundation of your leadership.

Leadership is not ultimately about skills, temperament, or personality. Obviously these factors affect leadership but they do not define it. Biblical leadership is defined by service (Matthew 20:20-28.) Jesus contrasted the worldly leaders of His day, how they lorded it over one another, with His call to His disciples to be servants of one another. The temptation for all of us is to make leadership about ourselves, to do things for our own benefit, and to build up our own image, power or control. Biblical leadership is always the opposite – it is about building others up and equipping them for works of service. How are you serving your team? What are you doing to help your team members be better ambassadors for Christ? How can you help them in their language learning, in their cultural adjustments? Are there specific things you can do that will set them up to succeed? A good team leader devotes himself to the well-being of his team members and he sees it as his job to develop them and address their needs. If you make serving your team your priority in leadership, you will most likely have a team that loves you and will go anywhere with you – not to mention a team that is effective in ministry!

Conflicts will happen on your team. They might happen between you and another member or they might happen between other members on the team. Expect them to come. Sadly, in my experience, many missionary team conflicts don't end well, and it is the rare leader who can make a conflict win-win rather than win-lose. To my great sorrow, I have seen leaders punish team members with whom they disagree. Usually the issue is not a black and white, cut and dry issue of sin, but more often it revolves around a conflict of personality, interpersonal issues, or ministry philosophy. There are many people who never go back to the field because of these conflicts and leave the field damaged emotionally. Unless there is a specific sin issue involved, resist the urge to be punitive. As a leader in a formal position you do have the authority to make decisions, and you may need to make some hard decisions. Sometimes you may not be able to resolve an issue – especially if it involves differences in ministry philosophy – but you can agree to disagree and if need be you can bless your team member to move forward to another team or situation. Don't use your authority to punish people with whom you disagree. A mature leader recognizes that sometimes there are incompatible working relationships and rather than making it win-lose (where one person is deemed the loser and another the winner), do your best to find a win for everyone involved. How you handle these situations will say a lot about your character.

Be open and honest, and loving in communication. One temptation for all of us is simply to avoid the difficult discussions that sometimes need to happen. When there is a conflict, sometimes it is easier to 'not go there', but usually that only leaves your team members feeling like you don't respect them enough to talk directly with them about a problem. No one wants to be left in the dark, guessing. In my experience, those you lead may disagree with your assessment of a situation or problem or your decision about something, but they will appreciate your honesty and your willingness to lovingly bringing up concerns you might have or to explain your decisions. Don't be passive. If you love someone you will move toward them.

Don't play favourites. As a leader you will likely be drawn to certain members of your team more than to others. This is normal, but make sure that every member of the team knows he is valued and has an equal voice. Do your best to treat everyone equally and fairly. Some team leaders end up creating a team environment where there are first class members and second class members. Those members who feel like the second tier won't stick around for long.

Be collaborative in decision making. There are two primary ways you can engage in decision making on your team. First, as the one with actual authority, you can make all the decisions for the team and then try to get everyone to follow you after the fact. Second, you can be collaborative and involve everyone in the process of decision making. I am not talking about small inconsequential decisions, but rather the big decisions that affect everyone significantly. It is much easier to simply make executive decisions (and sometimes that might be necessary), but from my experience, in the long run it is much more valuable to make big decisions in a collaborative way so that everyone feels they have had a voice in the decisions that are made. At the very least, never make big decisions that affect the team or specific members of the team without first talking to your team or the members involved. Collaboration is hard work, but it yields wonderful dividends in terms of team unity and team effectiveness.

As you lead, serve your team; make their needs and their effectiveness your priority! Be like Paul who said, "Follow my example, as I follow the example of Christ" (1 Corinthians 11:1.)

Sincerely,
Sarah Joseph

WEEK 1
Day 5

Coffee break with John

John Grace moved from his home in America to East Asia 16 years ago. He has been in been in leadership for 12 years, including team leadership and other organizational leadership roles.

Dear New Leader,

This must be a good day.

Most typically, conversations about leadership tend toward the burden of leadership or the challenges of leadership. Yet leadership is indeed a privilege and a responsibility that must be dispensed with a deep respect for those we lead, and the God we serve. Even as I write these words, I am keenly aware of my own deficiencies in this regard.

The U.S. military boasts of an all-volunteer force, as opposed to a conscripted one. Soldiers serve their country voluntarily, and receive compensation accordingly. For those who give up their lives on the battlefield, no amount of money could equal the sacrifice they and their families have made. So considering what is being asked of them, it would be ridiculous, perhaps even an insult to expect soldiers to pay their own way. "Who serves as a soldier at his own expense?" Paul asks rhetorically in 1 Corinthians.

Enter the world of full-time cross-cultural Christian ministry where people routinely volunteer, taking on risks to their own life, and the lives of their immediate family, all while raising their own financial support. In today's hyper-individualistic consumer culture, one would be hard pressed to find a group of people who have as much 'skin in the game' as these men, women, and children, despite whatever flaws they may have. Indeed, in this regard they have no equal.

Years ago, I was asked to take on a broader leadership role. The way I understood this was, "Would you be willing to love your friends by serving them in this way?" My spirit joyfully agreed, while the rest of me searched frantically for the nearest exit. And yet, by the grace of God, I committed myself to the task, continuing to take on the same risks and burdens of those I was asked to lead. The path we have walked together is sacred ground.

So whether you're having a good day, or a bad one, remember the tremendous privilege you have as you lead and serve your friends in an endeavor that will have ripple effects far into eternity. "Greater love has no one than this: to lay down one's life for one's friends" (John 15:13.)

Blessings,
John

Lunch with Cathy

Cathy Thompson is a second-generation missionary. Raised in the Caribbean by American parents, she has spent 23 years in Eastern Europe, 20 of those years in leadership, including team and field leadership.

Dear Leader,

I'm a unique leader in my mission organization. I'm a single (never married), 55 year-old lady and a TCK ('third culture kid'; formerly known as 'MK', missionary kid). I have an American passport but I grew up on an island in the Caribbean Sea and now I've served in Central Europe for over 23 years. I live in Hungary but, as an area leader for my organization, I've served teams in nine different countries, most in the former Eastern Bloc of Europe.

Wow, this letter could be really long, but I'll just try to hit on a very few thoughts.

Leadership, to me, means depending heavily on my Father to give wisdom, strength, and abilities to do the task. Actually, I see it as a lifestyle and not just a job. It doesn't stop when the sun goes down or on weekends. This means I need to be careful to make time for myself and my relationships with both my Father and others outside of the organization.

I wish I had known how consuming it can become if proper boundaries and practices are not set. I spent too many years almost killing myself trying to meet everyone's presented needs only to find out that there were even deeper needs that I never met.

I have loved developing dear, long-lasting friendships with those I serve, and feel as if I have a very large family. One of my great joys is seeing many I've served now in leadership and now walking the journey with them as peers.

Therefore, I'm just going to list things that I believe are important and have made my life and service much more do-able and rewarding.

Prioritize your time with your Creator and Lord! Only He can truly empower you to lead in a healthy way for the entire journey! Make prayer your lifestyle!

Set a realistic work schedule and then every six months evaluate it and make it even more realistic. What you think is realistic changes as the seasons of your life change. Do not be rigid, but make sure that you have scheduled time for family, friends and yourself, for whatever feels like downtime and time that renews you. Make sure you take time away. The work will always be there and there is always someone who can help your people while you're gone for a short time. Remember their Father is there even when you're not there. This is extremely important if you don't have a spouse or family who naturally cause you to step away at times.

See people as people and not tasks! We are made for community and relationships and that's what people need more than anything else. Listen!

When it comes to the challenging parts of leadership, grace without truth is just avoidance. Avoid avoidance; it will get you in a deep hole out of which it is very hard to climb.

Remember, you will make many mistakes; but if you have a teachable, receivable spirit you will grow, and those you serve will respect you.

Trusting God is much better than trying to please God! This takes the work out of your hands and puts it in His.

Replace the word 'commitment', which is a great word – with the word 'surrender' whenever you can. When you commit to something, the work and results are up to you. When you surrender to the Lord and a task that He has led you to do, the results are up to Him and the work is done relying on His strength.

Make sure you have a small community around you to whom you can go for encouragement, accountability, and mutual mentoring.

Understand that it is God who has called you to this position at this time; therefore, rest in Him and enjoy the journey. Revel in the ways that He chooses to show His wisdom and strength in and through you. Be overjoyed when you see His working in and through you.

I love many verses but there are three that the Lord has brought back to my mind almost on a daily basis all through the years. They are:

"You make known to me the path of life; you will fill me with joy in your presence, with eternal pleasures at your right hand" (Psalm 16:11.)

"But he said to me, 'My grace is sufficient for you, for my power is made perfect in weakness.' Therefore I will boast all the more gladly about my weaknesses, so that Christ's power may rest on me" (2 Corinthians 12:9.)

"The one who calls you is faithful, and He will do it" (1 Thessalonians 5:24.)

In closing, I'd like to say that I never dreamt that my Father would ask me to walk this journey. What a wonderful life I've had! What a joy to serve in a leadership way with my mission organization!

Serving with you,
Cathy Thompson

WEEK 1

Day 6

Coffee break with Jo

Joanna Lima was born in New Zealand and moved to East Asia 16 years ago. Joanna has served in various leadership roles for the last 15 years including team, field, and organizational leadership.

Dear New Team Leader,

There are so many things that could be said to you as you step into a leadership role, but there is one thing in particular I want to draw attention to. It's something that I've observed in many leaders in a variety of contexts, including myself from time and time. It is a tendency to think that we know best; that our experience, longevity of ministry, or even our role means that we are better able to discern what God is doing than others are. Taking on a leadership role does not mean that we are automatically equipped with more spiritual gifts than we were yesterday. Or that suddenly we have become infallible and we don't need the community of faith around us to minister to us just as much as we minister to them.

We trust that by the time people join a cross-cultural ministry team, they have been led by the Holy Spirit to do so, and that this has been confirmed and affirmed by their sending church. Of course this doesn't mean that they are infallible any more than you are! Many people come with life experience, spiritual gifts, ideals, and vision. Some of those things will be tempered with their experience of living overseas, particularly in their first year when we all struggle with our identity in a new place where we don't know language or culture. But as their team leader, do whatever you can to encourage and affirm the gifting that you see, and trust the Holy Spirit who resides in them just as He does in you. It's far too easy to squelch enthusiasm and vision with the 'realities' of what you've experienced or that you anticipate for them. And the longer you've been engaged in your local context, the more you may sense that you know better than they do.

My experience is that often our longevity in service can actually make us lose sight of the very things that others see when they first arrive on the field. Your job is not to bring new team members around to the reality (as you've defined it) of what they ought to expect or do. I don't mean to undermine the necessity of helpful orientation; there's no doubt that is critical. But don't lay your experiences or your expectations of what can and can't be done on teammates who are coming in with new vision, new aspirations, new gifting, and new perspective. It takes a lot of humility to listen well, and yes, learn from those who may well be younger than you, different from you, and newer to cross-cultural ministry than you.

Trust the Holy Spirit in those who serve alongside you. Be eager to seek His leading together. I am not talking about reneging on your responsibilities as a leader – quite the opposite. As a leader, know your own limitations. Know that you don't embody all the gifts of the Spirit. Affirm those teammates who bring a different perspective and who are differently gifted. Don't assume that you have to know it all, or do it all. It takes depth of character to be grounded and not threatened by others who may be more gifted than you, to celebrate their giftedness, and to seek together how God will use that gifting. For this season, God has called you into a leadership role. Perhaps one of your most important leadership functions is to call out the gifting you see in others. I'm so grateful for those who have done that for me, and trust that you and I will also do that for others as we lead.

Blessings,
Jo
Romans 12:6-8
2 Timothy 1:5-6

Lunch with Roger

Roger Menkim moved from America to Central Asia 10 years ago and has spent the last seven years in team and field leadership.

Dear Leader,

As someone who came to leadership very reluctantly, I want to share how leadership has enriched my life on the field and revolutionized my perspective on church planting.

In the part of the world where we serve, missionaries are inclined to be a little more self-reliant and autonomous. As a result, my early ideas about field leadership included the belief that it meant extra burdens on time – especially away from 'ministry' – and that it could also be superfluous, intrusive, bureaucratic, and overbearing to our workers. I was only slightly right.

Adding to my skepticism about taking leadership was my lack of formal training in it. Although I had supervised and managed others in various roles since high school, those experiences were not easy or fulfilling, nor were they what I would call successful. I made a lot of blunders. So, when my wife and I joined the organization, we let it be known that we would decline any leadership role. Rather than being meant to safeguard our own time and levels of responsibility, I intended it more as an attempt to protect the agency!

It has only been through the Father's providence and mercy that I have been able to grow through my mistakes and have my eyes opened even more to what He is doing all around us. During my first few months in my current role, I was carried through my foundering by the insight and generous support of more experienced leaders both within and outside our organization. I cannot thank them enough for their willingness to sit down with me and listen to my expressions of uncertainty, insecurity, and woe. Their encouragement and example helped me see that it was possible to serve in this role without constantly worrying about sinking the ship! Beyond this, two experiences with formal instruction strongly molded my views, but in different ways.

One of these was the formal leadership training process offered by our agency. It not only imparted some practical skills, but more importantly it set the tone for leadership in our organization by laying out priorities, including godly character and grace as opposed to an emphasis on quantifiable results. I could now speak with confidence when comforting some workers who lamented their lack of production on the field. These priorities also helped to distinguish between 'bad' and 'good' leadership in our context. For this reason, I was able to be reflective rather than anxious when I was once vilified for not being enough of a dictator!

The other formal experience involved starting Church Planting Movements (CPM). Towards the end of that week of training, the lightbulb lit up for me when the lead teacher told us that his approach to CPM was not primarily about church planting but about leadership development! At that moment, the many references to leadership in Scripture began to come together for me; the ways in which the Father has worked through flawed men and women to guide and save His people became more clear. Not only did my ideas about the discipleship of local believers change, but also my perceptions of the roles of workers on the field shifted. It was not enough for us to exemplify 'good Christian living'; we also needed to show good representations of leadership in order for local churches to grow in a healthy way.

From that time forward, I have sought to apply leadership lessons to discipleship and church. For example, I have learned to help others say no to leadership burdens they do not need to carry. If the Body exists as members with manifold gifts, why should we insist that each of us as workers all fit that 'ideal missionary' image? Mutual accountability, vision, and the giving and receiving of discipline are among several other important concepts that I have added to the framework in which I mirror our ex-pat community against the local church.

The importance of unity and community are vital principles in my new train of thought. I have always known that community is important in the Christian life, yet in regards to the workers on the field, it was close to being an abstraction. However, John 17:21 drove a stake into my irresolution: "that all of them may be one, Father, just as you are in me and I am in you. May they also be in us so that the world may believe that you have sent me." Immediately, unity became a necessity rather than an ideal. As a leader, it meant that unity in community needed to begin with myself and my family.

Of course, unity does not require that I compromise in order to work with people whose approaches I cannot in good conscience support or be associated with. However, it does mean that I should not just shrug my shoulders when someone feels that they need to leave a team just because they can't get along with teammates. That kind of conflict is not left simply as an interpersonal issue but now has a more eternal significance. Community is also important because I know that, as a leader, I daily need the prayers and support of those whom I lead.

In this role, I have been forced into doing many things I would not have chosen to do. This has not just been because I wanted to be a slacker in administration! As a leader, I have been faced with spending a great deal of time helping ex-pat workers through their challenges, sending some workers home and telling others not to come, and going against my own personality type by adding structure to my daily routine where I used to just 'go with the flow.' I have been blessed by having one of my co-workers step up to be my sounding board and accountability partner. He prays daily with me and gives me great counsel while listening to my concerns. When the burdens have been heavy, I have also been blessed by the affirmation and concern of others in our area.

Apart from the connections of community, I have come to see that these challenges have been God's will for me as well as for all of our workers because this is the way He makes us grow. Moreover, I know that if we only stick close to doing the things that we know we are able to accomplish in our own strength, we will fail to do and see the things that only the Father can do through us.

Consequently, I no longer feel that leadership is superfluous. I now see that it is a vital part of the way that God works in the church and thereby in the world. It has given me a greater appreciation for my own leaders, a greater humility and weight for my own role as well as a greater desire for leadership development among all of our workers. I no longer think that leadership is intrusive but rather see it as a linchpin for the accountability, mutual encouragement, and caring that permeate the communities of faith that should exist in all the places in which we serve. I no longer denigrate leadership as bureaucratic and overbearing unless I, myself, fail by falling into the pitfalls of rigidity and pride. There have been times when I have had to play the 'bad cop', but I have been reminded by Scripture in Psalm 141:5 and Proverbs 27:5-6 that true love is not characterized by hidden concern.

Still, one thing has not changed; and that is my perception that missionary leadership has shifted my family's time away from national friends (although not completely). This has been unavoidable but necessary. It has been good to be reminded by my own leaders that the time I spend with other ex-pat workers will, by extension, minister to other locals. Indeed, I am comforted by a vision of the parts of the body laboring together under His overriding will. I know that I and my family are not close to embodying all the gifts of the Spirit. We need others to grow and to do His work!

For now, this leadership role has passed to our home, and He has been faithful to help us work through the discomforts, missteps, and wrong attitudes so that we may be content with His will for us during this period of our lives.

Fortunately, leadership is one of those things that can be passed on. I look forward to passing the leadership role (and its lessons) on to others, not because leadership is a burden, but because that is part of the Great Commission. If His will is for us to be fruitful and multiply, we can be overjoyed at the opportunity to pour into others the gifts and grace He has poured into us through other brothers and sisters in Christ.

Grace,
Roger Menkim

Day 7

Day of Reflection...

Take a moment to reflect on the 'conversations' of the last 6 days…

- What portions of the letters did you underline? What struck you or jumped out at you?

- Is there anything you disagreed with or would like to have further discussion about?

- What themes seem to be standing out to you? How do these things tie together?

- Sit for a few minutes and ask the Lord, What would you have me walk away with and take to heart or implement? With whom would you have me discuss this?

Week Two

Week 2
Day 8

Coffee break
with Faithful Jade and Morning Dew

*F*aithful Jade and Morning Dew have led a team together in Indochina for the last two years. Originally from Singapore, these sisters have been on the field for 9 years with various leadership roles during that time.

Dear Leader,

Praise God for your obedience and faithfulness in serving the global Kingdom by taking up a leadership position. You have waited on the Lord for this, and we are thankful that you are in His will and purpose in this season of your life.

Walking in leadership is a sacred responsibility. You are also at the frontlines of a spiritual battle. You will be pressured on 'all sides' as the apostle Paul says – whether they are the 'simple' pressures of time and effort, or the far deeper gravity of affliction in our work, or tribulation in the family. Take time with the Lord, guard your heart, for it is where the Word of God is to reside, and it is your wellspring of life (Proverbs 4:23.)

As you walk in your leadership, the eye of your heart will be trained to be fixed on who God is, God alone, and to turn away from circumstances, persons, and even the pride and pity of self. Settle your mind on the things of God, and not of man (Matthew 16:23.)

You may have people on your team right now, in the very part of the world where He has placed you. He has woven your team together, and there is no mistake in the uniqueness of its tapestry and colour. God will use them to shape you in a way that will surprise you, especially if you have the privilege of serving with teammates that come from different nations and cultures. What a joy!

There is no better posture to lead from than as one who listens – to the Spirit of God, and to your teammates. We carry so many assumptions in the way we perceive and act. Even as you are unravelling the layers of understanding in your host culture, the same holds true for your team, be it from one or many cultures. But one thing is sure – it is definitely a multi-personality team! Perhaps the strongest foundation for a healthy team life is the solid friendship and relationship you would have taken time to build, borne out of recognizing God's call, travailing through challenges, and rejoicing in grace together.

As a leader, you will be called to be a peacemaker. Forgiving one another and encouraging forgiveness will lead you and the team to experience God's very rich grace as you "make every effort to keep the unity of the Spirit through the bond of peace" (Ephesians 4:3.)

The Lord's promise to you is that He will direct your paths as you trust Him. May you grow in faithfulness as you continue to act justly, to love mercy, and to walk humbly with our God.

Standing with you in hope and joy,
Faithful Jade and *Morning Dew*

WEEK 2: DAY 8:

Lunch with Todd

Todd Blankenship, originally from the USA, has been serving in Southeast Asia for the last 10 years, many of those as a team leader, and is now serving as a field leader.

Dear Friend,

Perhaps you're feeling a little overwhelmed at the idea of becoming a leader of missionaries; or on the other hand, maybe you've been thinking it's about time someone called you up for this role? I remember when I was asked to move into leadership: I felt a mixture of confusion, panic, and excitement. The leadership meetings at the time were being held in Bali, and I took the bait because who wouldn't want to go there?!

I remember the first meetings: sitting around the room were people with so much wisdom and experience and… age. I was a boy among men, and there were some there in the room who wanted to make sure I knew it. I definitely knew it. In fact, just being asked to give you my thoughts on leadership brings back some of those feelings – insecurity, doubt, pride, inadequacy, confusion.

My mentor, the one who asked me to step into leadership, said something to me that I've never forgotten. "There are things I think the Lord would want to teach you about that moving into leadership may help you learn." It was genius! I mean, at that point, how could I say no?! But it was true. And I've been saying it to those that I've asked to step into the role ever since.

Seriously, though, as I look at leadership and my journey in it, I become more aware of my short-comings and my inadequacies. I think this is a product of my pride. The reason I think that is because I very quickly begin to think about my strengths and weaknesses, my abilities and gifts, and the areas in my life where I tend to do poorly, as the measure for my performance or worth as a leader. Sadly, I usually look at those things as the primary decision-makers when I'm asked to move into a new role or take on new leadership. It's pride because it really is all about me – even about the stuff that I'm not, but that I wish I was...

Leadership is a great crucible: it has the potential to alert us to so much of the junk in our lives that we need to change. And because of that, it's a beautiful, beautiful thing. I mean, if we are serious about killing sin in our lives, a leadership role is a very effective tool. I don't have to beg the Lord to point out the sin in my life very often, because something always comes up in my experience as a leader that alerts me to my sin. But the thing is, sometimes becoming aware of my tendency to be prideful or self-absorbed is exhausting, so I just stop thinking about it. I indulge the thought that I'm pretty good at what I do, or perhaps I even dwell on how inadequate I am. If I allow myself to coast down that river, it doesn't go well ...ever. When I'm honest, I understand that leadership is much less about what I'm good at and what I'm not good at, and more about loving and serving people.

Another great quote from a mentor is that leadership is basically about two things: (1) love God, and (2) love people. My tendency is to make it about so much more than that, and in so doing, I make it so much less than it could be. As you can see, I don't have any original thoughts. But take the advice of my mentor: remember that leadership is about those two things.

You will be busy in leadership, but do not neglect your relationship with the Lord. Don't forget: the Kingdom work that you are striving to see Him do among those you serve is the same Kingdom work that you desperately need done in your own heart. You need to spend time with Jesus! You need to fall in love with Jesus. It's so easy to begin to see your job and your relationship with the Lord being sort of the same thing ...but they are not! Don't fall for that trick of the devil. Keep the Sabbath! Linger with the Lord. Love Him with all your heart, mind, soul, and strength. Make this your first priority in leadership. See to it that your own heart is soft enough for the Lord's work to be done on it. And see to it that you recognize the voice of God when He speaks. In order to do that, you need time with Him. Take it!

When I worked in a hospital, we used to joke that work would be so much easier if it weren't for all the patients. Well, regarding leadership in missions perhaps we could say the same thing: leading would be so much easier if it weren't for all the people we have to lead. It's very easy to become cynical or to begin to see those in your leadership sphere as projects, people that you need to change. Sometimes we can even begin to look at those we lead as tools to get a job done, and we treat them like objects we need to sharpen and maintain for the work. I have slipped into this mentality too often, and I have created many problems and much pain because I have stopped seeing those in my leadership sphere as brothers and sisters, created in God's image, who have value (inexpressible) way beyond what they can do for me.

I have seen the strategic element of leadership push me toward manipulating people rather than loving them. We can cloak things in spiritual missionary language and talk about it like it is 'empowerment', but I believe that this kind of 'spiritual' or strategic manipulation is evil. And it can be so subtle. For that reason, I spend plenty of time looking at Jesus. His leadership was life-giving! He actually empowered people! His example helps me to see the subtle ways that I sin. And though this is a rebuke in a sense, it is a glorious rebuke! After all, I don't want to be a jerk! I don't want to be, yet I often am!

So, here's where the words of my mentor seem to really be coming true: there are things that the Lord wants to teach me that leadership will help me learn. I am learning about loving people, and love is essential in leadership! And it is essential in following Christ! I'm not great at it, but when I'm getting really upset about something one of those I'm leading says or does, I try to ask myself, "What is going on that is getting me so bent out of shape?" Usually, I find that it has more to do with me than with the other person. Usually I'm upset because I feel like I'm not being appreciated, or treated fairly, or respected (read: put on a pedestal) – all of which are about me. It is so easy to go deep into the pit getting those selfish needs met in a leadership relationship rather than really serving and loving people. I find I am constantly digging that hole.

My organization, Pioneers, has a core value of 'Participatory Servant Leadership'. This is the value that I come back to most often. I suppose it's appropriate since it is about leadership. I find myself reflecting on it a lot, not because I 'get it' or because I model it so well, but because it is the way Jesus led, and it is the way I want to lead. The thing is, becoming a servant is what we are all called to, not just those of us in leadership. However, the beauty of leadership is that there is this 'built-in' accountability to show us what it means to serve. And so, leadership is a tool God is using in my life to teach me to learn to become a servant. And I'm sure He'll use it in that way for you, not because you specifically need it so badly, but because we all do. And I'm grateful that the Lord has put this in my life (and now in your life) to help me (and you) to become more like Jesus.

Hey, there are a couple of other quick things, since I'm writing you, that I've found helpful:

Spend time being with the people you lead. Try to have more than just a business relationship with them. Take them out for golf, or even a movie, or whatever. Learn about them …and that kind of learning is usually best done while you're doing something else.

1. Don't talk about how busy you are with those you lead. It can communicate to them that you don't have time for them or don't value them.
2. Love your family: your spouse and/or your kids. See to it that they know they are the most important people in your life. You may have to learn how to measure how well they know that. Sometimes asking them isn't really the best way.
3. Find ways to give positive feedback to people. If possible, do it in public.
4. Seek and offer forgiveness quickly.
5. Take a vacation.

Well, that's an awful long letter from someone that claims to not have anything to say.

For God's glory,
Todd Blankenship

Week 2

Day 9

Coffee break with Dave

*D*ave Carter, originally from America, has spent the last 12 years on the field. The last six years have been spent leading a mission team in Chad.

Dear Leader,

Starting a new team among an Unreached People Group (UPG) is a blessing that I'm excited to see the Lord call you to. It is also a road filled with landmines. It's a path that will in all likelihood be more of a refining process for you and those you lead than it will be about establishing God's kingdom among a UPG. Having been in your shoes before, there are a few things I've heard and that helped me, and some lessons I've had to learn the hard way that I hope you can simply learn from my mistakes. The following is some advice I'd like to share, for what it's worth.

You need your team to lead. While I was a team coordinator, working on recruiting for a team, I heard a speaker describe leadership as having three spheres: vision, administration, and shepherding. For everyone but Jesus, we fall short in some respects in at least one of those spheres. We need our teammates to help fill in our leadership inadequacies. The sooner we discover and acknowledge our weaknesses, the sooner we can rely on our teammates' giftings to get the job done. This is a crucial way to build trust in a team.

If you don't have trust, you don't have much. Our solid rock is Jesus Christ, and in missions teams we hold that in common and should rely on that unity daily. This does not, however, guarantee a high level of trust among teammates. Trust comes over time. As a team leader, one of the best ways to help foster it on your team is to model it. Be transparent with your teammates, and trust them.

Expectations need to be verbalized. In my team experience, everyone simply wanting to initiate a Church Planting Movement (CPM) among a UPG did not mean we were all on the same page. For example, what 'CPM' meant for one person wound up being very different from another. These differences of opinion came to a head in a team meeting that resulted in tears, frustration, misunderstanding, and long-lasting hurt. Verbalizing expectations rather than assuming them is only going to serve the team. Finding ways to ask questions and talk about topics in order to draw out these expectations is one of the most important things you can do as a team leader.

You are a servant. Christian leadership is a service job. It can be a thankless job, too. You will be discouraged from time to time; you will feel misunderstood by your teammates; some days you will want to quit and get a job mowing grass. In those times remember this: "the Son of Man did not come to be served, but to serve, and to give his life as a ransom for many" (Matthew 20:28.) Preach it to yourself. Ask your Father in heaven to make it a joy for you to follow in the unsung steps of Christ. He sees, and remembers!

The team that prays together is successful. If anything, as team leader your job is to encourage your team to pray in the kingdom. This is the most strategic part of being a team. If you don't do it you risk ministering in your own strength – among the unreached this is a recipe for deep disappointment and frustration.

Finally, I offer this prayer on your behalf: Lord, bless this new leader with wisdom beyond his years. Give him a humble heart, ready to repent and ask for forgiveness from his teammates, and just as ready to forgive in Jesus' name. Give him the heart of a lion and the skin of a rhino. Give him guile to recognize and thwart the schemes of the enemy aimed at dividing and killing off his team. Lead him to paths of righteousness for your name's sake. Through him and his team, Father, glorify your name, let your kingdom come, and make them more like your Son.

Your friend,
Dave

Lunch with Christophe

Christophe Aleti has been serving as a church leader in his home country of Togo for 12 years. During the last three years he has also been leading a mission team there.

Dear New Leader,

The following are some of the lessons I learned in team leadership and would like to share with you:

A leader must have a clear vision. There is no leadership without a clear vision. A leader must have a vision and share it with his members so that they can take ownership of this vision. If you do not have a vision or if you are not able to explain your vision to convince your team to have ownership of this vision, you will not succeed and you will lose the respect of your team; they will consider you as incapable and will even try to lead you. In sharing the vision, the leader must be ready to accept input from others to improve the vision so that it will become a common vision. The leader must define the role of each member who must complete it and make reports; if not, as a proverb says, "The work of everybody is no one's work."

Respect of the hierarchy is very important if you want to succeed in your ministry – even when you don't agree with your leaders or are in a time of open crisis with them. You must respect them; obey them while you are trying to solve the problem. The respect of hierarchy also means respecting your immediate colleagues. A leader must respect the members of his team; they also must respect him. It's not good for a leader to deal with those who are under other leaders without them being informed. He must love his team members and defend them when necessary. Loving them means to encourage them, to congratulate them, to assist them in case of need, to be with them, to visit them. In short you must give them consideration, never minimise them, but consider them.

Be open with them and involve them in decision-making. It's often a slow process in decision-making but it is very important if you want others to take ownership of the decision and commit to it. The advantage is that if your members are informed and involved in decision-making, there will be an atmosphere of trust; they will not doubt or suspect your management. Rather they will take your defence when a problem arises. I myself experienced it; several times the members of my team have taken my defence. They could not do so if they did not know what I'm doing. But you must clarify the situation at the beginning and let them know in what areas consensus decisions must be made and where you can act alone. If you do not do it at the beginning, they will believe that you cannot make decisions without them. They will rise against you on the day that you take a decision without consulting them. This is very crucial in my personal experience; if you do not clarify this situation at the beginning, you will have problems with your team, you may be led by your team, and you will have frustrations and blockages in your leadership.

Maintaining the unity of your team is a key element – I would even say the secret of success in team leadership. A leader must work hard to maintain this unity; if not, he will fail. To achieve this requires certain qualities from the leader – namely, the humility that brings you to see yourself as their servant and not their boss. A good leader must be prepared to pay the price, to make sacrifices to keep the unity of his team. Some situations can cause tension, frustration, but the leader must overcome; he should not keep anger or hatred against his members. Rather if there is a problem he must resolve the dispute as soon as possible.

Confrontation is a key element in the management of crises. It is sometimes difficult, but it's beneficial; it can concern the team as a whole or individual members. A leader must be able to confront team members when they do not act well. The purpose of this confrontation is to bring unity and serenity in the team. We should not punish the offending member without having confronted him, without giving him the opportunity to explain what he did. But if you don't know how to proceed, the confrontation can degenerate and not give the expected results. But confrontations, if properly managed, will strengthen the discipline in the team and will avoid such behaviours. The confrontation may be oral or written. In my case I use both, depending on the situation. I use the oral confrontation if the problem is not very serious and written when it is serious or if the person is re-offending. In my experience, the member becomes more aware and takes it seriously when the confrontation is written; that is to say, a note is sent to the person concerned stating the shortcomings or mistakes he has made, and recommendations, that is to say, what to stop doing and what you expect of him from that moment. After a note is sent to the person concerned, you must meet him and give him the opportunity to explain what he has done. But this time should not be a moment of tension; you must control your emotions so that it does not degenerate. If the person continues after that, you can meet in the presence of some people in your team.

A leader, especially a young leader, must learn from the experiences of his seniors. To succeed in his leadership, the young leader must learn from his elders or through reading books on leadership, or by going directly to seek advice at home. Personally, I received a lot of advice from my elders, especially in times of crisis or decision-making. Without the advice of my elders, I would have cracked and maybe resigned during difficult times. It is also good to seek someone's advice – it can be your mentor or someone else – when you want to make an important decision.

Any leader, and especially young leaders, must be prepared to face pressures, disappointments, and frustrations. The pressures come from your leaders, from the requests or needs on the ground, the needs of the families, and mail to process. Disappointment is often due to lack of understanding and collaboration of your team members and lack of support of your leaders. Sometimes people don't see the sacrifices you are making; instead of encouraging you, they will fight you. All this can create frustration, so that one can be led to wonder if it's worth continuing.

Because of multiple occupations, the pressures and the increasing challenges that you face as a leader, sometimes you do not have time for your friends, family members, and even for God. The time you should spend in spiritual activities is sometimes reduced in the face of your responsibilities. At this time you need to be careful: you're on a slippery slope and you have to redress the balance.

Another danger to be avoided by the leader is to manage only certain sensitive spots and especially the finances. Do not handle money alone – that can tempt you; you have to charge someone to do so, but under your authorisation and supervision.

Grace to you,
Christophe

Week 2

Day 10

Coffee break with Mel

Melissa Parenty, originally from Australia, served as a missionary and team leader for eight years in Southwest France.

Dear Future Leader,

When I think about leadership on the mission field, my experiences revolve largely around the concept of leading transparently and vulnerably. It was not my choice to lead in this way (I am an introvert who loves her privacy!). Rather, this style grew organically as a God-initiated by-product as I pursued obedience to God's calling on my life.

To live transparently and vulnerably, allowing people access into my real life to learn from me up close and personal, was not an easy step for me. I preferred that people saw my 'good' side at all times and that I had everything under control so that they would be impressed.

However with a missionary husband that I was being a helpmate to, seven children to care for, ministry and business going on 24/7 in our home, my life was full-on busy, noisy, stressful, exhausting, and regularly chaotic. To let people in to see everything laid bare was risky …they would see that in the busy-ness I regularly forgot important things, witness me in my pyjamas at 11am, overhear our marital arguments, see our kids fighting with each other, hear me calling out to my children to clean their skid marks off the loo and pick up their dirty socks, and see me drink a glass of red wine at the end of the day as a tribute to myself that I had survived, and to psych myself up to face the next.

However, I obeyed God and opened up the door of my life, and started leading this way more. The feedback was amazingly encouraging. People love to learn from real life. Either they see you do something well and think, "I will imitate that" or they see you struggle or perhaps even witness your failures and think, "I will learn to do that differently."

Either way, they are blessed by your willingness to let them share your journey. They are deeply appreciative of being allowed into your life to experience it at a grassroots level. People told us they learnt from us lots of cool things that we often forgot we were modelling …the big family fun vibe, a marriage that stays together, practical faith in action, joy in the noisy chaos (games, worship times, meal table), how to make time for fitness and sport, how to be an engaged parent, how to run a business as mission, how to set healthy boundaries, how to manage the never-ending tension between juggling busy schedules and keeping God at the centre, etc.

I really encourage you to lead transparently and vulnerably …it is an exciting and authentic way to impact the lives of those learning from you.

Grace to you,
Melissa

Lunch with Dan

*D*an Taylor first moved to Central Asia 16 years ago. For most of his years on the mission field he has served in various leadership roles including team and field leadership.

Dear New Team Leader,

    I don't know you; but then again maybe I do. I was you once, and in some ways I still am. Maybe you are one of the rare exceptions in our line of work: a tried and tested leader who is beginning this role with enormous amounts of wisdom and experience. My guess is that you are not. You probably are closer to what I was when I started: a twenty-something idealistic missionary, with a couple leadership gigs under my belt but with less knowledge than I had opinions … though I wouldn't have seen it that way. That is not to knock who I was or who you may be. We all were there. Hopefully we don't all stay there. It is not a place to be despised. It is, however, a place to grow from.

    I am not a know-it-all. I certainly have no desire to come across that way. All I can do is share from my experience and what God has done in my life in mission leadership. If He uses that to touch something in your life as you start this journey, great! If not, also great!

    In this past year I've been introduced to a new person, a person who is really a conglomeration of a lot of western missionary leaders. I was introduced to him through a good friend who named this conglomeration 'Johnny (or Jane) Confident'. I realize as a conglomeration he/she is a stereotype, and yet, stereotypes are there for a reason, and Johnny is present because we have all met him. In some ways, maybe we all find bits (or more) of ourselves in him.

    I mention Johnny in part because it is likely that either you are already just like him or that you will be very tempted to become like him. Johnny comes to the field full of motivation, energy, strategies, methods that work, and more… ready to win a town or a people group to Christ. In some ways, nothing is wrong with Johnny. In other ways, everything potentially is. Any one characteristic we find in Johnny isn't bad in and of itself. In fact, some of it is admirable. The question isn't the characteristic itself, but the source or motivation behind the characteristic. Does the characteristic arise from the flesh – a desire to succeed, to prove oneself, to amount to something – or from the Spirit, from God-given intimacy and energy? For Johnny it is the former. For most of us it isn't that simple. We are most likely a tangled mess of the two sources. Thank goodness. It's this mess that keeps us humble and puts us in a position to be living out and wrestling with the very gospel we desire to be messengers of.

The movement from being Johnny to becoming ourselves takes a lifetime to complete, but it is a journey we need to be on if we are going to truly be effective mission leaders. I can't map out the journey totally. Each of us starts from a different place and travels different terrains. But our end is the same. We arrive at our home: Jesus Himself.

Though I can't map out every detail, I want to share with you some of the navigational signposts that have become important for my journey …one I'm still very much on.

God has brought us to the field not because he needs us. He will use us, but primarily He wants to use the field to do something in us.

Intimacy and unity with Christ is the basis for our ministry. We are so tempted to pursue 'good' things, strategic things, in the flesh. Instead we are to be like Jesus who "spoke just as the Father told him" (John 12: 50), moving in ministry while yoked to the Holy Spirit, listening to Him and doing what He tells us to do.

Be honest about our weaknesses. Don't let shame be a stronghold in our lives. Cooperate with the Spirit, believing that He is about finishing the work He has started in our lives (Philippians 1:6.) Engage in hope, rather than retreating to denial or giving in to the delusion of pride.

Community/team is not only a support for our ministry but a means by which it comes. In John 13:35, Jesus indicates that the quality of our community will be an apologetic that points to Him. Investment in team is an investment in the ministry.

Again, these are just tastes of some of what God has done in me. I trust that as you walk His journey for you, you will taste more of the freedom of being His. I hope that you will find His grace sufficient as you move into mission leadership.

Grace,
Dan

WEEK 2

Day 11

Coffee break with Ben

Originally from Australia, Ben Axemann spent 11 years in East Asia, the last eight years in leadership. He is currently involved in supporting ministers and missionaries from his base in Australia.

Dear Friend,

You may be the kind of person, like me, who loves to help people work for unity, and generally doesn't end up in conflict themselves. This is a blessing, and a gift. But for many of you, like me, it also comes with danger. Sometimes we have developed these skills and careful sensitivity to the state of mind of others in part because we have feared conflict for a very long time. Perhaps our whole lives. This is part of the "fear of man," described in Proverbs 29:25. If you have an unhealthy fear of conflict you will know it: a passion for avoiding conflict, a dread that conflict might occur, and for me worst of all – the horrible sick feeling in the stomach when conflict has come upon us despite our best efforts. And as one struggling with a fear of conflict, you are sometimes going to be tempted to make decisions that are about you, and avoiding conflict, rather than about God's glory and Kingdom.

But don't worry, you're a leader, and you will have an abundance of opportunities to grow in this area! How will God grow you? By letting you land in situations where your fear of conflict is activated, yet asking you to lead in directions that will not make it go away. There are times when godly leadership is deciding something that makes you very unpopular with some of those you lead, and you will be put to the test. If you have that sick feeling in your stomach

– stay the course! So long as you have carefully sought God and His wisdom, and along with Him searched your own heart (because you never know what lies there sometimes), then stay the course! That horrible sick feeling may just be an opportunity to grow out of the fear of conflict – and move on towards the fear of God, which is the beginning of wisdom (Proverbs 9:10.)

Grace in your journey,
Ben

Lunch with Andres

A Mexican-American dual citizen, Andres Herrera Vazquez has been serving on a team reaching out to the Tarahumara of North West Mexico since 2010. In 2014, he became a mission team leader.

Dear New Leader,

Here are a few lessons on leadership that I would teach myself – if I could go back in time – which I gladly share with you as you step into leadership.

First, ask and search for help. I don't know what it is with many of us serving in leadership – perhaps it's that a number of us are over-responsible first-borns; perhaps it's the discernment to see areas of need or windows of opportunity that others don't initially see, or the passion for a God-given vision; perhaps it's our personality and our personal story, or a mix of all these. Though most of these are God-given gifts to serve in leadership, along with these there may be the idea that, as leaders, we should be the ones caring for and directing others and not being a burden to our followers (though some leaders do burden their followers financially or otherwise). We may also be haunted by that devil-inspired stereotype of the leader who always has his act together, who has all the answers, wisdom, and skill, who never shows weakness or need as he rides into the sunset. But whatever it is, the fact is that in the end, many of us just don't ask or search for help like we should in our lives and ministries.

Although it's true that many times while serving in leadership we will have to take steps on our own to open a path or change course, there is also a subtle yet very destructive temptation to continue to go it alone for an indefinite period of time. It is also true, especially in the cross-cultural missions world, that many times we can be more efficient just getting things done by ourselves rather than sharing about a need/opportunity, seeking help, and then training the helpers (when necessary); but one very important Kingdom principle to keep in mind is that efficient doesn't usually equal fruitful.

When we don't ask for help we feed our pride and create a persona that is not truly who we are down deep inside, which in turn exposes us to a great deal of temptations and sets us up for failure. It's very sad to see the all-too-common case of the Christian leader who is exalted by his followers to an unhealthily elevated position only to fall scandalously later on. He shares in the fault for not resisting it and intentionally humbling himself; maybe he even encouraged it. Acknowledging and exposing our areas of need to others – being prudent about it, both in the deep and superficial – and asking for help, keeps us in touch with our real selves, keeps us open to others, and in a safer spiritual walk.

When we don't ask for help we distance people from us, for who can bear being close and vulnerable to someone who seems self-sufficient or super-mature? We lose many opportunities to bless and be blessed by others in our personal lives and ministries. Contrary to what many believe, exposing the flaws and needs in our personal lives and ministries may actually encourage others in their walk with Christ and His service and bring unexpected help and blessing to our own lives and ministries. It's humbling and surprising to find out how many people are better at certain ministries than us and how many have a maturity in their walk with God that can help our own walk with Him.

When we don't ask for help we rob people of their opportunities to participate in ministry; we may create a ministry elitism by making it look like only certain specially called and specially equipped people can serve God like we do. In the Christian world, this has created the terrible clergy vs. layman classism in which thousands of Christians believe the lie that only spiritual leaders truly serve God. In the missions world we may keep thousands of

God's children believing that all they can do for the Kingdom is pray and give occasionally; when in reality every Christian is given particular gifts and a personal role to play in the advancement of His Kingdom among the unreached.

Through the years, a number of godly leaders have taught us that life is messy, true spirituality is messier, and relationships are the messiest. God has designed for His Kingdom to grow in our personal lives and in this world through the inter-dependence of the parts of His body; and serving in leadership, we are one of those parts, never apart from the body. Is it not amazing to see what God has done starting with 12 men that He (the Almighty, truly Self-sufficient, Eternal God) asked to join and help Him? Not asking and seeking help from our brothers and sisters both in our personal lives and ministries will always end up being bad leadership.

Second, listen, listen, listen… Oh how easy it is while leading people to quickly form an opinion of them and then to swiftly pass judgement on the motives behind their actions! This is especially true when they behave in a way or say things that hurt or disappoint us (generally more common than we'd like) and create conflict. We may observe patterns recollecting some past experiences, hear snippets of information here and there, use our powers of observation and deduction or refer to their assessment packets, and using all this infallible evidence, judge and even sweep them out of our favor.

But as uncomfortable and awkward as it may be for those leading people (especially if they're goal-oriented and unskilled in deepening relationships like me), there is nothing like having a good sit-down to ask important questions seeking to hear people's hearts. Oh, how much easier it may be to tackle a near-impossible ministry obstacle than to solve conflict while trying to help someone under our leadership sort out his/her heart!

The process of biblically resolving conflict will generally include us also baring our hearts and sharing how we feel about the situation, being careful not to push our perspective over theirs (which is very easy due to the fact that we're leaders), but rather asking the right questions and listening... a lot.

What comes out of this may be as simple as a misunderstanding or as complicated as a turbulent past with many unresolved heart issues. Whatever it ends up being, there is good reason for Christ's challenge to Peter, the leader, to show his love to Him by 'tending' His flock; and this challenge applies to us as well. There is no exhortation in Scripture for leaders to produce great ministry results; rather we are to care for those God has placed under our leadership.

You see, in the end we will give account for those whom God placed under our leadership because they are not, and have never been, ours. They are His and one of the main reasons He temporarily placed us together is so that we will help each other grow, even in conflict, and continue fulfilling the plan God designed for our lives.

Finally, you have to decide if you will be a 'Lid' or a 'Trampoline'. My pastor once shared the concept of 'Trampoline Leaders' and 'Lid Leaders' which he had read about in a John Maxwell book on leadership. 'Trampoline Leaders' are the ones who help people get to a higher level in life and ministry than when they arrived under their leadership, even if it means being surpassed by them (in a good way). On the other hand, 'Lid Leaders' set themselves and their personal limits as the limit (or lid) for those under their leadership, not allowing people to surpass them in any way.

It got me thinking and wondering: "What is my leadership style? Have I ever used that terrible cliché, 'That's fine, but this is the way we do things here.'? Or do I allow and encourage others to express their unique gifts and potential as they seek to serve God, even if they're different or better than me? Do I feel in competition with them or threatened in my position by them? Or do I acknowledge that I and the ministry are being completed through them? How do I feel when someone who has been under my leadership is being called to a different or even higher position in their life and ministry?" (Much more so when it means losing a valuable helper.)

Truly, when Peter, the early church leader, wrote to other Christian leaders not to lord over the flock of God but to tend it willingly, he was also thinking of this aspect. For the lives and salvation of each person in the flock were never paid by their church or ministry overseers but by the precious blood of our Supreme Leader. Consequently, the potential and direction of each one should not be determined by the overseer and his petty ministry plans, but by the design prepared for each one before the beginning of time by the Great Artist and slowly revealed by Him as He finalizes His masterpiece of Salvation in this world and time. As overseers, we will give account to Him of how we led and what we did to serve those under our leadership, including helping them reach the potential God gave them and following the unique path He has laid out for them.

Grace to you,
Andres

Week 2

Day 12

Coffee break with Sandro

Sandro Oliveira and his wife have more than 15 years of experience in mission in their home country of Brazil, in the Middle East, and now in the United Kingdom where he leads a mission team involved with church planting among unreached people groups.

Dear Future Leader,

Despite having been a team leader for approximately four years only, I worked as the 'right hand man' for the team leader of another missionary team I was part of while working in Brazil. The team leader was an American missionary and he was seen as a very good leader. I really learned a lot just being close to him and seeing him leading from a servant point of view. He really modelled the servant leadership style found in Jesus. It was not a weak leadership; he had authority but never imposed it. He knew how to be firm and I don't remember seeing him complaining when the other team members let him down. I am saying this because working with him helped me to learn and develop leadership skills that are very important to me today.

I really think that anyone considering leading a team should first be part of a team themselves. They should experience team life and know what leadership is and is not. I know that not everyone will have the blessing of having a good leader as I did, but even if the team leader is not as great a leader as he/she should be, I still think someone aspiring for leading a team could learn a lot by just being in a team and walking close to their team leaders.

To be a team leader is not easy at all. It is a task that demands a lot of wisdom, patience, organisation, and most importantly God's anointing. Another important factor to consider in my opinion is that in an organization where there are very few policies and guidelines in place (like my organization, Pioneers), leading can be quite challenging. A team leader in such a context needs to be able to dialogue, find consensus, and make compromises. As a team leader of a group of very experienced missionaries, I had to learn that leading meant to hear a lot and almost always to make concessions to what I thought was the right thing to do. Even though sometimes I felt I had lost by not having my way, in the end things worked really well. The team today has grown both in number and in service. There is a sense that we are all in this together and we see God using us in many different ways. Looking back, I am confident to say that I don't think we would be in this position if I had pushed to have things my way. For sure, some people would have left.

One thing I didn't know when I took the leadership role was that when you are a team leader you have much less time to do your own ministry. I kind of heard this being said, but I really didn't grasp this until I was facing challenges regarding time…or rather lack of time! Leading involves quite a bit of administrative work and lots of communication to do. You also need to allocate time to think and reflect on the team vision, team members' well-being, dealing with relationship issues among team members, team activities, etc. You have to be sure that this role is what God wants for you for this season. This will help you see that your ministry is also the ministry of the others you are leading. That it is not so much about what you can achieve, but what the team has achieved that matters.

Another very important thought here is that I believe we team leaders need to be accountable to our own leaders. You want to model the standard of this to your team members. I intentionally keep my leader informed and aware of pretty much everything we are facing as a team. I often talk to him and listen to his advice prior to important decisions or team meeting discussions. Another benefit of keeping a transparent line of communication with your leader is that when a team member decides to go and complain to him of something he or she disagrees about, it is of no surprise for the leader. I had this happen to me once; my leader knew of the issue beforehand, so when the team member came to him he was fully aware of the situation.

Lastly, I would like to say that we need to be humble to learn from our mistakes and improve what we have done well. In this area, reading books on leadership is very helpful. It is also important to take part of the leadership trainings. I have learned a lot from our organization's leadership programme. Taking part of the training was one of the most important events in my life and ministry. It helped me to grow closer to God and to lead from a servant point of view. It also gave me important skills and tools that helped me lead in the way that pleases the Lord and encourages people!

May you be blessed,
Sandro

Lunch with Jeffrey

Jeffrey Chan, originally from America, has spent the last 15 years on the islands off Southeast Asia. He has been leading a mission team there for the last three years.

Dear Future Leader,

I am thankful for this opportunity to pass on the mantle of leadership to someone as capable, godly, and trustworthy as you. As you prepare to embark on your journey in leadership, please allow me to testify about the journey our faithful and gracious Lord has led me through, in the hope that it may be of some help to you.

From my years of experience being a follower under other people's leadership and, more recently, as an appointed mission team leader, spiritual authority is what I would point to as the essence of good mission team leadership. By this I mean that leadership is about living life before the Lord in such a way that others see something that they want to imitate. It is also about speaking in such a way that others hear something that rings true (biblical and backed by life example) and that they will therefore want to follow in the direction we set as a leader.

I can testify that my effectiveness and fruitfulness as a leader has been directly related to the degree of spiritual authority I may or may not have been receiving from the Lord because of either my ability or failure to live wholly unto the Lord.

In order to continually receive that spiritual authority from God, pace-setting needs to be happening in my life as a leader. If I'm not setting the pace in the things that I'm asking or expecting others to do, my credibility and spiritual authority will be diminished and questioned. For example, if I ask my teammates to tirelessly invest in the life of believers and unbelievers, but I'm not doing this myself, my words will ring hollow. Some of the key aspects of life and ministry in which I need to be setting the pace are:

A growing intimacy in my relationship with Jesus. Loving God: consistent, quality time in the Word, prayer, worship, and other spiritual disciplines (fasting, solitude, etc.).

A growing passion for the brethren. Loving the saints: fellowship, praying with and for, mentoring, discipling, empowering/enabling, teaching, equipping, and serving.

A growing passion for the unreached. Loving the lost: praying with and for them, serving, leading them toward discovery of gospel truth and learning about Christ (evangelism).

In order for some of the more private aspects of life to become more visible to others, it's important to do life and ministry together. I must invite teammates into my life and my family's life (celebrations, outings, recreation, etc.). I must also plan to spend time with teammates personally (man-to-man) and in community.

Some examples of activities that can be done together include: Bible study and discussion; topical or book study and discussion; prayer fellowship meeting; prayer walks; fasting and prayer; personal devotions (have a shared personal devotion time with one or two teammates); team retreats; family vacations or day outings; attending a seminar or conference; evangelism; service projects and other serving opportunities; planning and carrying out training seminars or similar events.

There are a few other leadership lessons I've learned…

Plan, be ready, and be willing to give lots of time and attention to new teammates. Some will need more time than others, but plan and allow for the upper limit. The first six months are critical to the development of a strong, healthy relationship with new teammates. Some key aspects to work toward are: open, consistent communication (availability), building trust and interdependence (avoid one-sided dependence), imparting skills and knowledge.

Seek to understand and learn how teammates are 'wired' – their passions, gifts, talents, personality, and experience. Guide them toward the team's vision and mission, but don't force them into long-term roles and responsibilities that will drain them. Be willing to agree to part ways and move on (even going off the team) if it turns out that the fit isn't right after giving it due time and process.

One thing I've heard about team leadership that I disagree with is that new team members should not be allowed to contribute or participate in team ministry planning because of their lack of field experience and knowledge. I believe that they should be invited to participate in the planning process with the understanding that they are not required nor expected to contribute, but are encouraged to ask questions and even offer advice or counsel. This allows them to feel part of the team's life and ministry from an early stage and helps them learn from more experienced members as plans are discussed and formed. The new team members who have chosen to attend such meetings have often helped bring a fresh perspective to the process that has benefited the team, not to mention that it has helped them get a jump on the learning curve.

Another thing I've heard about team leadership that I disagree with is that scheduling fewer meetings is somehow always good or better than scheduling too many. Some of the current thinking stems from the need to cut down on the number of ineffective meetings and also to free up team members' time to engage in their core ministry activities; but I have found that a consistent reticence, resulting in difficulty scheduling necessary and helpful meetings, betrays a lack of commitment to the team's ministry.

Thanks for the opportunity to share with you some of the lessons I've learned from the examples of those who have served me so well as leaders and also from the opportunities the Lord has given me in leading others. It's only because of His grace and guidance through the Word, the Spirit, and the fellowship of the saints that I am able to convey this testimony. I am confident that He who is faithful will also build on the work He has started in your life and bring to completion the testimony of your own journey in leadership.

In His grace,
Jeffrey

Week 2
Day 13

Coffee break with Linda Smith

Linda Smith and her husband were born in America but have spent nearly all of their adult lives in Asia. They have lived in East Asia for nearly 20 years where they served as team leaders for 10 years.

Hi Leader,

As I reflect on 19 years of serving overseas, I realize I'm just beginning to understand what I've learned. It hasn't been a linear process of learning skills and knowledge and then becoming a leader. Instead, leadership has been a mutual, inseparable, daily following, listening, and dying to self as I live and serve in community and let the Spirit do the ministering.

Jesus lived out and spoke out following, listening, and dying to self in community. In John 7:16 the greatest servant leader proclaimed to His followers, "My teaching is not my own, it comes from the one who sent me."

A new family had just arrived on the field, so I thought, "Ok, I need to pass on all I've learned." I remember admonishing them to make sure they take time to rest as a family and as a couple. I reminded them, "Ministry is 24/7 and will never be finished." Yet, did I live it out? Not nearly as much as I needed. I soon saw this family follow our example; giving out beyond capacity. True leadership came out of living it. And as a side note, this business of serving-never-stopping was just my pride in thinking I was doing the work rather than Christ. It takes me back again to John 7:16, "My teaching is not my own."

I love the African proverb, "One person can go fast, but a community will go far." In the beginning, my pride got in the way of listening and serving in community. I liked to do my tasks, then invite people into my sanctioned 'discipleship time'. However, real life leadership and discipleship happened as I invited my team and local friends into my daily everything: prayer, cooking, cleaning, shopping, studying and teaching the Bible, disciplining and teaching my kids, even listening retreats, and sharing with neighbors. I have heard so many moms on the field say they always feel guilty about being home or ministering too much. There is a constant tension. Yet I believe as moms, we lead churches and communities as we bring others into our daily life. Of course this still looks different in every family and marriage!

So I will continue this lifelong pursuit of listening and leading in community as I follow and die to self. The work of God is to hear what he says.

Linda

Week 2 : Day 13 :

Lunch with Todd

Todd McGaffen moved to Southeast Asia after many years as an elder in churches, pastoring in a large church and planting house churches in America. Todd has been leading a mission team for five years.

Dear Leader,

These ideas about leadership and the team leader role are based on what I consider to be the best aspects of a mission organization which make it possible to follow biblical models in the mission field. I have personally tested many common leadership ideas in the business world, the church, and the mission field; and in my experience these ideas have been of questionable value. God's Kingdom works very differently from the business world where most leadership ideas have developed. I have found the models of Jesus, Paul, Peter, and others to be the most useful in the field. For team leaders working out on the edge, biblical leadership models are of primary importance.

The ministry modelled by Jesus and the apostles centered on very simple and informal teams in which the leader did much more than just follow leadership principles. When we look at their lives we can see a few leadership concepts. But we see much more. We see prayer, waiting on the Holy Spirit for direction, discernment, gifting, and brave people willing to risk their lives because of faith. These are the most important things but they are outside the scope of traditional leadership concepts.

In these biblical models the leaders lived lives more difficult than anyone else. They did not have structural authority. They only had spiritual authority. Believers under the influence of the Holy Spirit recognized the leader's role and worked alongside them. There were no budgets, no bank accounts, no hierarchy, and no security. Instead there was much prayer, much ministry, travel, some spiritual discipline, release to start the next home fellowship or to send the next apostolic team. With this simple model they changed the known world.

Most mission organizations have budgets, bank accounts, and a hierarchy. However, in support of its mission in the field, some organizations have delegated authority for ministry all the way down to the team leader. Wow! Apostolic teams with authority to direct their own ministry ...that sounds like Paul's team. This means we can read our New Testaments and actually see how these teams worked.

Many are not sure what to do with the term apostle. But, following a biblical model, missions teams should do some of the kinds of things that the apostles did. We need teams of brave and prayerful people who are willing to wait on the Holy Spirit to direct their focus, perfect their character, infuse their gifting, and carry them along in their ministry in difficult places. In this ministry they need protection in the spiritual battle, healing from hurts, sickness and injury, direction in each spiritual discussion, discernment as they establish the church, and wisdom in the face of opposing authorities. Paul's team lived in this world. They were entirely dependent on the Holy Spirit, each other, and the churches that they planted.

Paul, as the spiritual head of this team, worked the hardest, suffered the most calamity, and had no wife or home. He had no official position but he had a spiritual role as an apostle for which he never apologized. Other people would sometimes question his role but his team and his churches saw it clearly. He proved his role and calling by making the biggest sacrifices, spending much time in prayer, going to difficult places, confronting the authorities, establishing the church, and setting apart the elders.

Some modern Christian organizations divide the labor: the home office worries about budgets and government regulations, trains potential missionary candidates, provides health insurance and other financial and emotional support. This leaves the team leader free to focus on what matters in the field. What a privilege and a responsibility we have to do this well.

If Jesus, Paul, Peter, and other New Testament ministers model the kinds of leadership we want in our apostolic teams, then we have many important New Testament examples of how we are to operate in the field. Here are some examples that I think are most important:

New Testament leaders spent lots of time in prayer. This is a requirement of anyone who understands that God's Kingdom is different than the kingdom of the world. Peter understood this and we get a glimpse of his lifestyle in Acts 10:9b, "Peter went up on the roof to pray." Like Peter, we need personal prayer in order to be connected with God, refresh our hearts from the sins and difficulties of life, keep ourselves from being caught up in the world, and to seek His direction. We need to pray corporately to get our hearts aligned, understand God's directives in the long term and for each specific day, have discernment about the threats and discouragement of the spiritual battle, and to become expectant to see the Holy Spirit do His Kingdom work in our midst, as we follow His leading.

A team leader must be the first to pray, model prayer for the team, and call the others to personal and corporate prayer. This is fundamental and comes before all other activities. I sometimes think that of all the Christians in the world those of us from the Western evangelical world are the ones who have the weakest prayer lives. Thus, prayer is a challenge. For those of us leading apostolic teams we must learn to pray.

The New Testament verse about leadership that I find most useful is 1 Corinthians 16:12, "Now about our brother Apollos: I strongly urged him to go to you with the brothers. He was quite unwilling to go now, but he will go when he has the opportunity."

Why is this so important? It shows how Paul along with his team followed the lead of the Holy Spirit. Paul was clearly the senior of his team. He wanted Apollos to visit the Corinthians. In fact, he "strongly urged him" to visit. However, Apollos said he did not feel led to go at that time. Paul accepted his answer because he knew that Apollos, like himself, was following the Holy Spirit. Paul did not attack him or try to control him. He did not say that he was able to follow God more clearly than Apollos. This was an apostolic team and he needed the whole team listening to the Holy Spirit as they did their ministry out on the edge where God had called them.

Apollos respected Paul's sense of the Holy Spirit as well and replied that even though he could not come now, because Paul felt it was so important he would come later when he had opportunity. This is an important example for apostolic teams doing the difficult work to which God had called them. They need to work as a team, having confidence that each is following the Holy Spirit in the heat of ministry and as plans are developed and often changed.

Paul talks about gifts, functions, and service in the community of believers. I call this our role. The Apostle Paul knew his role. He was an apostle and he never apologized for his role. He boldly did the work of an apostle.

Paul lists the typical roles in the community of believers in Romans 12, 1 Corinthians 12 (two lists), and Ephesians 4. He knew the role of his team members and blessed them to do the work. For example, Paul recognized the significance of Titus' role as an overseer in appointing elders and teaching, and gave Titus a number of important tasks. In Titus 2:15 Paul tells Titus, "These, then, are the things you should teach. Encourage and rebuke with all authority. Do not let anyone despise you." Members of an apostolic team need to know their role in their community. They need a blessing to operate boldly as they follow their calling.

It is important that the team leader know what role his people have so that the evangelist can be blessed and released to do his work. The person gifted in administrative work is blessed to do that. The overseer is blessed to do the work of an elder. Much effective ministry will be done if the team leader is able to discern and bless those roles on his team.

Paul and Barnabas confront each other in Galatians 2:13 and Acts 15:39. Barnabas, the encourager, confronts Paul about Mark at the end of Acts 15. Barnabas in his role sees the calling and potential in Mark; Paul does not. Verse 39 says, "They had such a sharp disagreement that they parted company. Barnabas took Mark and sailed for Cyprus."

Here, Barnabas has an opportunity to continue to travel and do ministry with Paul. He recognizes the authority of Paul, but he also understands his own role. Barnabas is so comfortable in his gift as an encourager and his discernment about Mark that he is willing to separate from Paul. Later, in 2 Timothy 4:11, we see Paul found Mark to be useful in his ministry showing that Barnabas' discernment was correct. We do not know for sure, but it is possible Barnabas saved Mark's calling and usefulness by unapologetically operating in his own role and confronting Paul.

In this example, Paul fails to trust the gifting of a member of his team. Barnabas acts on the leading of the Holy Spirit and makes the difficult decision to separate from Paul. Yet, in spite of the failure the moment, Paul's team was better in the end because of the gifting of Barnabas.

The team leader has the challenge to value and trust the gifting and discernment of all members. If we make a mistake we must be able to make it right, as Paul and Mark did in this first century story.

A difficult yet important role of an apostolic team is to confront unhealthy leadership in the church. In 3 John, Diotrephes is confronted because he likes to put himself first and does not acknowledge the authority of the apostles. In verse 10 John says, "So when I come, I will call attention to what he is doing, spreading malicious nonsense about us. Not satisfied with that, he even refuses to welcome other believers. He also stops those who want to do so and puts them out of the church."

Controlling and unhealthy leaders sometimes cause problems in the church in the Western World, so it's not a surprise when we encounter similar problems in the church in the countries where we serve. When team leaders are a bit older and have served for a long time in a country, they often have the authority in the community of believers to address issues that no one else can confront.

Sometimes local culture does not allow a senior person to be confronted, yet the long-term missionary can reach across that cultural issue. John confronted Diotrephes because the locals could not stop this controlling leader. When the culture makes following biblical models difficult, the long-term missionary can help adapt the principles to the local culture.

An apostolic team is a real challenge. The work is inherently difficult or else many would do it. The most important things are outside the scope of traditional leadership concepts. As leaders, we have been released to do this ministry and build apostolic teams. Therefore, we scour the New Testament looking for models and answers to the difficult issues we face when working as a team leader.

Grace in your journey,
Todd

Day 14

Day of Reflection…

Take a moment to reflect on the 'conversations' of the last 6 days…

- *What portions of the letters did you underline? What struck you or jumped out at you?*

- *Is there anything you disagreed with or would like to have further discussion about?*

- *What themes seem to be standing out to you? How do these things tie together?*

- *Sit for a few minutes and ask the Lord, What would you have me walk away with and take to heart or implement? With whom would you have me discuss this?*

Week Three

Week 3

Day 15

Coffee break with Tiffany

Tiffany Jackson was born and raised in America and moved to the United Kingdom to engage in mission to unreached peoples five years ago; she was invited to lead her team just under one year ago.

Dear New Team Leader,

As you take on this new adventure – and I'm sure it will be an adventure! – I pray that it will be joyful and wonderful in ways that you can't even fathom. As someone who has just started this adventure, I fear that I might not have much to offer you. On the other hand, the lessons might be that much fresher as I've experienced them over the past few weeks and continue to live them out. There are three lessons that stand out to me about age, service, and the greatest challenge to your leadership.

As a young leader, the first thing I can say is forget about age. Whether you are young or old, age doesn't matter. If you are young, you may feel too young and inexperienced to lead, but you have been chosen for such a time as this, and you have the great gift of spending the rest of your life learning to live well and apologizing when you mess up. It may seem awkward that you are leading people who are older than you, perhaps who have even been in the ministry longer than you've been alive. It's ok to feel that way. It will keep you humble. Just remember that your age is rarely relevant to whatever issue is at hand. In addition, just because people are older than you doesn't mean they have it figured out. Don't expect that of them. They've just had longer to make bad habits, obtain more hurts, and carry more baggage. Help them carry those things and don't give up on them.

Secondly, decide that discernment is one of the best things that you can invest your time in. Proverbs 4:7 says that you must get wisdom at any cost. This can be found in many ways from reading books to taking classes. However, the best wisdom I have received was from asking people questions, listening, and then spending time with the Lord. So many times we get obsessed with the idea of servant leadership that we lose sight of what that service looks like. We serve our teams by being there for people, doing the accounting, cleaning the dishes, and putting in the long hours. Those are all good things. However the best way we can serve our team is by seeking the Lord's discernment, hearing His vision and path for our team, and interceding for them. Don't serve just the physical, momentary needs of the team, but recognize that sometimes the best way to serve them is by going before the Lord.

Finally, as you embark on this adventure you are probably thinking of the many obstacles and challenges you will face. Perhaps you are thinking of the people group you are trying to reach, the challenging language that you're still trying to master, or the random bunch of personalities that God has placed on your team. But those things won't be your greatest challenges. Yes, you will spend hours praying for a breakthrough amongst your people group. You will spend many an evening frustrated over why your team can't seem to act like a team. But at the end of the day, the greatest challenge to your leadership will be you.

You see, I became a team leader in the midst of relational crisis. I was given a hurting and hopeless team amongst whom I was one of the hurting. I knew it would be hard. I knew my team didn't like each other and were as different as could be. I thought that they would be my biggest challenge. But becoming a leader was like holding a mirror up. Suddenly I could see where I let them down, where I lost my patience, or where I failed to lead well. My biggest challenge is me! My biggest challenge is laying down my pride and choosing to serve and operate as a team even when I'm the one who feels hopeless. My biggest challenge is nursing the wounds of my team first before nursing my own. It's not a tough ministry situation that I have to overcome, it's my own human situation.

So remember leader, forget about your age and the age of those around you – it's not really relevant; serve your team by seeking wisdom at all cost, and recognize that you will be your biggest challenge. But be patient. All of these things will take time. But God has called you for such a time and place as this. "Do not be afraid; do not be discouraged, for the LORD your God will be with you wherever you go" (Joshua 1:9b.)

Adventuring with you,
Tiffany

Lunch with Jim

*J*im Fredericks, an American, has been in leadership more than 40 years. He spent five years leading a mission team and planting a church in Southern Germany.

Dear Leader,

I'm so glad to hear of your transition to leadership. I'm glad your leaders see the potential in you that I do. When I think of the possibilities for you as a Christian to bring the presence of Jesus into missions leadership in very natural ways through your life, it excites me …and is why I'm writing.

Leadership is a hotly debated subject today. The cry is "Where are the leaders?" Amazon.com will pull up over 18,000 books if you type in 'leadership' as a subject, many with conflicting advice. Where can you and I go to discover what authentic leadership is? For me, Jesus has given me the very best answer with His classic teaching on leadership in Matthew 20:20-28. I call it "20/20 Leadership Vision." This short, pithy passage is well-worth long hours of meditation. It exposes the same faulty leadership philosophy in vogue today; that is, one that relies primarily on a top-down, position-based, expert-driven leadership authority (it's not wrong …only partial).

Two of Jesus' 1st century leadership apprentices, James and John, had bought into this incomplete leadership model of position as the primary basis for vision. Jesus challenged them to reorient in three ways in this fascinating exchange toward the end of His earthly ministry. Jesus' Aunt Salome comes to Him with her two sons, Cousin James and Cousin John. Auntie Salome and her two boys unabashedly ask for the top posts in His Kingdom, right next to Jesus Himself (see Matthew 20:21 and the parallel in Mark 10:35-45).

What is your response to their brazen request for positions of authority? The thundering sons of Zebedee had the taste of power on their lips and wanted for themselves the positions of authority and honor, of recognition and visibility. Many of us are scandalized by the raw-edge of their ambition, shrinking the Kingdom down to 'me-centered'. Their insatiable thirst in the first century, even if camouflaged with pious words, is to be first and over. "Give us position and place; give us influence and visibility; give us an office with the power of the expert." I would have been spitting mad, too, just like the ten.

But not Jesus!

Jesus sees the heart's desire behind their misconceptions about leadership influence. Although He does not give an inch in their campaign to grasp position-based authority as their basis for value and worth, at least they verbalized their distorted belief system about leadership. Now Jesus could then bring clarity and correction to sharpen their spiritual vision in three sweeping statements; so give them their kudos.

The first clarification is about suffering and sacrifice (Matthew 20:22-23a.) Jesus never dodges the hard realities. He exposes their false belief system on leadership, "You don't know what you are asking." In order to deal with our false or incomplete beliefs, our hidden idols, Jesus points to one of His sharpest tools: suffering.

Suffering, represented by the cup, and the larger, parallel response of sacrifice, go hand in hand with authority to influence. What a tragic lack of perspective they had with their overconfident, "We can." They immediately overcommitted themselves with their can-do response of individualism. But Jesus knew what lay ahead. Jesus needs battle-toughened influencers to further His Kingdom, and suffering can be a very effective teacher. Sacrifice is part and parcel of advancing the Kingdom. "Yes, you will suffer like me," because influencing others comes with a high cost. Pay particular attention here: Tough times often expose hidden idols that we love more than we love Jesus – a black hole into which our lives collapse from time to time. The solution is not behavior modification or a 'sin-management' strategy to protect us from the idol. Get to know Jesus better! Knowing Jesus destroys counterfeit idols, which only thrive when we feel we lack something within.

The second clarification is about sovereignty (Matthew 20:23b.) Positions of responsibility and authority are not theirs to grasp, but His Father's to give. God is the ultimate Promoter. Position, power, and popularity are all dangerous idols for leaders, so Jesus minces no words.

Today's common leadership philosophy profiles potential candidates more on the measurements of the outward than on the deep call of God on our lives. Preparation comes through schooling, past accomplishments, passing a battery of tests, giftedness and/or a special so-called leadership personality. Society pulls us toward the outward. We then lead on our terms, even while the Son of Man draws us to lead from what He has formed deeply within. Only the power of the Trinity can do this. He is God and we are not. Become His 'presence persons'.

The third clarification is about service (Matthew 20:24-28.) Finally, Jesus radically redefines true greatness. He first exposes the ego-centered attitudes of the other ten disciples. Jesus then calls His community of emerging leaders together. "Let's huddle up together!" Trinitarian leadership is always about T-E-A-M (Together Everyone Accomplishes More): community, togetherness, collaboration, and connectedness.

'Team' is God's original design, since He is the original Team-of-Three: the Father, Son, and Spirit. Since a Team of Servants rules the universe, how much more crucial to foster a team of influencers in every aspect of life, in the family, in the church, and in our work world. Team and koinonia (community)-based leadership is not some new, 21st century add-on. God designed us in the image of community, T-E-A-M, like the Triune God Himself.

So, why did Jesus come to earth? What is His mission statement? He closes this passage by concisely explaining His mission so we can also adapt a similar focus for our own.

Jesus came "to serve and to give his life as a ransom for many" (Matthew 20:28.) He laid down His life on a daily basis (to serve), but also in a unique, one-of-a-kind act (to give his life as a ransom). His deliberate life purpose was to model and to reveal a revolutionary style of life and leadership (to serve), and also to restore intimacy with His Father as the only source of such a life (to give his life as a ransom). We write books about the latter, the essential and necessary salvation Jesus provided through His unique, one-of-a-kind death. However, we often overlook the revolutionary style of life and influence Jesus modelled: to serve others.

Since Jesus is the Model of humanity for His image-bearers, then we too are called to make our lives a gift towards other people, giving ourselves without expecting any direct return from those we serve. Jesus shares the amazing sufficiency of His Triune Community-of-Three with us. Then God's people can in turn experience and pass along this rich, Trinitarian relationship and resources with others. Your department can then become a living, Trinitarian eco-system with an amazing network of interconnectedness and a wide range of spiritual nutrients …an island of life in the midst of a secular business. This rich community soil is adaptive, creative, and dynamic in nurturing and releasing life to the ends of the world, just like the Trinity. God calls you to this 'garden plot' to be a thermostat, setting the temperature and not just measuring like a thermometer (to confuse word-pictures!).

So, how do you view Jesus in the Gospels? As the impossible ideal because He is God and we are not? Or as the best possible model for our lives because Jesus walked fully as a man while on earth (while never ceasing to be God – oh mystery)? The first robs us of the perfect model of Jesus, the second Adam, who shows us everything on God's heart for created humanity. Leadership, Jesus' revolutionary style, is not an impossible ideal today; it is the best possible model to relate to each other and to the work-world in a way they can never imitate. The first view leaves us without any sure foundation on which to build our lives. I have based my life on the second choice: Jesus as the best possible model in every aspect of life.

You are an image-bearer of the Triune God, and God Himself has made you adequate for this task before you. Such influence and leadership is within the reach of each of us who long to experience deeper koinonia in community since God designed us to serve, influence, and lead. Service is the single most intrinsic trait of healthy leadership influence. The Trinity models for us the perfect expression of unique giftedness and individuality in interdependent community, our purpose as leaders. This will astound the world (John 17:20-23.)

I've purposefully written a longer letter today because this move into leadership launches such an important season in your life. I will be praying for you for '20/20 Vision', that you become a revolutionary leader like Jesus, sowing the very presence of Jesus into your people as you train this team toward excellence.

Your loving friend,
Jim

Week 3
Day 16

Coffee break with Kevin

Kevin Smith, originally from America, has spent the last 20 years of his life in East Asia, 10 of those years as a mission team leader.

Dear New Leader,

I have one main principle to share with you as you begin your leadership journey.

As leaders – or believers – we should never do anything alone, unless we absolutely cannot avoid it.

We are sheep. No matter how much we think we need to be responsible and face up to Goliath alone, we should never do anything alone. This is extremely hard for leaders to implement because they either can't find someone to go work together with them (for several reasons) or they don't even think about bringing someone along with them.

I'll share just a few other brief thoughts with you.

What does it mean to be team leader? It means that while you are often in the 'storming' stage with new people you will need to absorb a lot of frustration from them as they are 'born' into a new place.

I wish that I had known, when starting out, that my leadership role may be unending, lonely, and frustrating. Although I say this somewhat in jest, be aware that if you are not careful, you may be led into depression or other pitfalls. If I had the chance, I would have given myself freedom to step down and take a breather after three years; even if that meant we would have no team leader.

A few important lessons that I've learned include the truth that God is always good, and He will be with you, He will teach you, and you will become more like Him.

Some of the successes that I've seen are witnessing the stability of a team (members and/or leader) that is sustained by His power, which seemed to allow space for establishment of His work. It takes time to set up the temporal (family, office, school, hospital) while He builds the eternal (changing lives, building the kingdom). Sometimes others have gone before us (and the Spirit has gone ahead too) and did some of this work, so it takes less time; but it always takes a long time.

Grace in your journey,
Kevin

Lunch with Dave

Dave McGilligan, an American, has been focused on ministry to the Arab world for 34 years. During that time Dave has served in a number of countries and capacities, including team, field, and organizational leadership.

Dear New Leader,

My main leadership thought is about the importance of developing self-awareness in our leadership. Insights about self-awareness can involve personality, family upbringing, culture, and education. Being self-aware means that we are in tune with who we are as people, and how we influence others through our beliefs, values, and behavior. In the leadership setting, being a self-aware leader means that I understand my approach to leadership – my leadership style, my expectation of those I lead, and the effect that my leadership has on others.

For example, if I am a reflective introverted leader, a significant amount of my mental processing will take place hidden from the view of others. When I share ideas and thoughts, it could feel like I have already made up my mind (which in some cases might be true!). Those I lead may feel excluded, expressing comments like I am controlling, non-inclusive, or isolated.

Being self-aware means I know my style, but also the preferences of those I lead. Being self-aware would mean in this situation that I acknowledge my normal way of behaving, but that I consciously seek in team life to accommodate those who are different from me. While each of us has a preference, leaders are called to function in both dimensions. Through focused intentional development, we can grow and compensate for the skills that do not come naturally. However, no one will excel in all areas, so we also need to rely on others with complementary gifts and skills that we are not naturally gifted with.

Enough about personality preferences. These examples are very short and pithy, but I would encourage you to explore more in understanding personality preferences. A Google search on 'MBTI' (©Myers-Briggs Type Indicator) will offer further help.

Another self-awareness tool that I find increasingly helpful for interacting with others is the 'Johari Window'. Once again, a variety of websites can provide more detailed information. This simple tool involves four windows into our life: open, blind, hidden, and unknown.

The 'open' quadrant involves those things I know and others know. In a team setting, that quadrant comprises all the information and insights we know about each other: our personality, gifting, life journey, shared vision for ministry, and the agreed way of living and working together. The more that is shared in the open quadrant in team life, the easier it is to live and work together.

We all have 'blind spots' – those areas of our attitudes and behavior that others see but are not as apparent to ourselves. Blind spots could be silly little habits of twisting our hair or tapping our feet. It can be the gruff manner in which we relate to others. Sometimes a blind spot can be an area of strength or gifting that is not readily clear to self, but which others see more clearly. Having our blind spots identified and brought to light can be painful, but hugely beneficial if we are committed to growing.

The 'hidden' quadrant involves those things in my life that I do not readily communicate to others. I may withhold information out of fear, from perceived lack of safety, or simply because I do not know how to articulate some of what is stirring in my mind and heart. The hidden quadrant may involve personality (I am a reserved person who does not freely share openly), culture (my culture may be one that is reserved or less divulging about personal matters), or family upbringing (how we were raised sets the tone for how we live in our adult lives).

The 'unknown' quadrant is that part of my life that is only fully known by God. The dysfunction, inner baggage, and inner wounds we carry in life are not always clear or understood to ourselves. God knows this area of our inner world, and at different times in our life, the truth of the Word and the work of the Holy Spirit will bring clarity to some of these unknown areas. Healing can flow from increased understanding. The words of the psalmist in Psalm 139 are an invitation to God to delve into the unknown quadrant and bring understanding and insight. "Search me, O God, and know my heart; test me and know my anxious thoughts. See if there is any offensive way in me, and lead me in the way everlasting."

These brief reflections are only snippets of topics that can be unpacked in much greater depth. The basic encouragement of this letter is to make self-awareness a life-long learning pursuit. Keep growing in your understanding of how God has "fearfully and wonderfully made you" (Psalm 139:14.) Remember that your strengths can also be a weakness when taken to the extreme. Keep in mind that some people you lead will have differing preferences and personal or cultural values. What is natural and valued by you can either be welcomed or resisted by others. Be yourself and exercise your gifts under the Spirit's leading, but be aware of the diversity and differences around you. If you do so, you will grow in self-awareness.

Your brother on the journey,
Dave

Week 3

Day 17

Coffee break with Jim

*J*im Billson and his wife are originally from America. They served 13 years in Kazakhstan and one year in Russia, and were team leaders for approximately 10 years of that time.

Dear Brothers and Sisters in Christ,

Greetings! I hope this is helpful in your seeking His will for your life.

We served as team leaders for two organizations during our years on the field. Our first team was multinational, comprised of 13 men and women from three countries. Our second team was comprised of Americans. While, our third team was comprised of six nationals with my wife and me as the only Americans.

In some ways, serving as a team leader is like serving as a pastor of a large church. There are so many demands and functions that the team leader is responsible for; it can become overwhelming. Over my years as team leader I've made many mistakes, and it is from those that I think we have the greatest opportunity to learn.

First, I would say that keeping your personal walk with the Lord the top priority is critical. Being a team leader is so demanding; it is essential that the power of the Holy Spirit is the power source, otherwise burnout will be imminent. That means daily prayer time and daily time in the Word needs to be kept on the top of the list. Second, since there are so many 'jobs' that the team leader must oversee, it is important to delegate to others – especially areas that are not your strongest gifting. While in Kazakhstan, we started our own business. Unfortunately I had to be the head of that business as well as being team leader. It would have been better if another team member could have taken on the role of managing the company, leaving me more time for team leading.

Next, as team leader, one of the main roles is mentor and coach of your team members. I would set up weekly individual meeting with each of my team members to see how they were doing, how they were growing, dealing with their language and culture learning and their personal ministry.

I found that when team members experience culture stress during their first 12 months in country, sometimes they transfer their stress to other things (i.e., their house) or to other people (i.e., their team leader). In that situation they think, "If only this one thing was different, then everything would be fine." If you, as team leader, are the target of their frustration, you will need 'thick skin'. You will need to be patient with them, and help them understand that they are experiencing culture stress.

Having regular worship times together as a team will be critical for bonding, release of stress by giving it to Jesus, and mutual support. Having weekly worship times together would be ideal. Our team made this as a goal. Being a mission worker is very stressful, and being a team leader is even more stressful. Having healthy methods of dealing with stress is critical. Living overseas for us required a lot of walking, so that gave us a fair amount of exercise, which is also important for stress management.

It is impossible to cover all the topics necessary for being a successful team leader, but I would go back to the first point – keeping the Lord first. God never asks us to do more than we can handle or accomplish. Sometimes we put more stress, requirements and expectations on ourselves than God does (at least I do). I have to remind myself that my first responsibility is to sit at Jesus' feet and be His disciple.

May the Lord bless you and encourage you as you serve Him as a team leader!

In Christ,
Jim

Lunch with Keith

Recently retired, Keith Fraser-Smith and his wife have served a lifetime in missions in the Arab world. During that time, he led a variety of teams in a variety of contexts – large and small, mono-cultural and multi-cultural, mission and church based teams.

Dear Friend,

Greetings in the Name of the Lord Jesus, our servant King.

In 2012, I was asked to speak briefly at a leadership training retreat about how culture had been played out in my leadership. As you embark on your own ministry of leadership, I wanted to share these reflections with you also.

A leader is not culturally neutral. As soon as I stand up and open my mouth it is usually obvious where I come from. My physical appearance, my clothes, and my age contribute to invoke different cultural expectations from my team members. The more you are culturally aware the more you will see yourself in perspective and the more you will be able to communicate appropriately and in multifaceted ways. You may have been 'appointed' a leader after a thoroughly 'democratic' process but that doesn't mean you are culturally neutral.

A leader needs to know their own culture and character. It is very helpful to have some understanding of the stereotypical beliefs, values, and behaviour of your own culture. Also comprehending, however limited, your personality and appreciating your life experiences and how they interrelate with your cultural inheritance is a lifetime's reflection but necessary, especially in leading multi-national teams.

A leaders needs to be aware of cultural differences related to decision-making and conflict resolution. You will soon pick up that different cultures handle these situations in different ways. I recommend the writings of Geert Hofstede to you. In what he calls 'high power distance' cultures, decisions tend to be dictated while in 'low power distance' cultures, consultation and consensus are more common. Individualist societies, predominantly Western, can be in your face with the 'facts'. 'Truth' may come through the process of dialectic: thesis and antithesis. Because of the honour and shame dimension of collectivist societies, predominantly non-Western societies, conflict is normally dealt with by a third party. If you are the leader of a multi-cultural team you need to identify who that person might be if there is a conflict. I was once in a conflict with a brother from a Middle Eastern culture and it had to be resolved by the intervention of the mission's international director and the chief executive of the person's mobilising base. Asian cultures make decisions in private and then they are ratified publicly. Some cultures 'lobby' and some are very 'diplomatic'. You will benefit from knowing the cultural decision and conflict resolution styles of your team members and juggling them, always seeking fairness, justice, and reconciliation.

A leader needs to understand status and/or achievement. In the Arab world, I have always benefitted from grey hair (now white, some say). Grey hair is a sign of age, maturity, and wisdom in many collectivist societies, and such people are automatically respected. In individualist societies, academic attainment or business acumen – the American dream – bring respect and honour. Traditionally, British 'class' society gave precedence to 'professionals', who may or may not have academic credentials or wealth, but who had 'standing' in the community. I experienced frequent emotional conflict as I moved between different cultures. One moment I was being honoured and shown great respect (e.g., in South Korea), and the next moment I was being questioned and sometimes ignored because I only have a BA (Bachelor of Arts) degree and a post-graduate diploma.

I shall never forget being invited to a reception for Sister Teresa of Calcutta in Amman, Jordan by the Jordanian Minister of Tourism (if I remember correctly). The portly Minister spent almost seven minutes listing all Sister Teresa's global accolades. When he eventually finished she turned to him and standing diminutively beside him said graciously, "You have forgotten one thing. I am first and foremost a servant of Jesus Christ." Our status is only in Christ, regardless of whether our culture emphasises status or achievement.

A leader needs to navigate national rivalries. National pride normally demonstrates loyalty to the country where we are born and to which our behaviour, values, and beliefs normally default. (Remember that there are always exceptions to this rule.) Without such commitment, countries would fall apart. However, when that loyalty is expressed in blind nationalism, then a multi-cultural team leader can have challenges, especially if there are already national rivalries between the two or more disputants. However, the wise route is to prevent such conflicts before they appear by good biblical teaching on the fact that we are first "fellow citizens with God's children" (Ephesians 2:9/Romans 9:8) and "one in Christ" (Galatians 3:28.)

A leader needs to be aware of communication issues and uncertainty avoidance. Never enough can be written or said about the complexity of languages and the potential for misunderstandings between people of different cultures. I recommend you always check and double check what is meant, especially if what has been heard appears to be offensive. Tone and volume can be deceptive too. Some cultures discuss issues as though they were at war with you and others so quietly that it is easy to ignore what is being said. I have been accused of not fulfilling what I agreed to when I was only gathering information. As a result, I try to remember to tell people that I have heard their point of view (often clarifying it) and that I will take it into account when making a decision.

A leaders needs to be cautious with humour. Only in exceptional circumstances and by exceptionally well-loved and respected team members should jokes ever be told in a multi-cultural team context. Our humour is so nationally and regionally nuanced that it is not worth the danger of offense and the damage it can cause to relationships. Even humour at the expense of the teller is not recommended. It may be one thing for a British team member to make an understatement, which we all laugh at, but another thing to deprecate themselves in a joke.

In Christ, your discipleship mode as a team leader is to be grace-filled, modelling holiness, trustworthiness, love, servanthood, attracting respect, demonstrating sacrifice, and behaving consistently. On the godly strength of these relational qualities, a leader in a cross-cultural team context will negotiate with their international colleagues regarding team matters, seeking cultural accommodation within the unity of Christ's body. Unless there is an unequivocal biblical reason why an action is sinful there will be no right way, just different ways, of doing things.

"Make every effort to keep the unity of the Spirit through the bond of peace" (Ephesians 4:3.)

In Him, the Good Shepherd
Keith

WEEK 3

Day 18

Coffee break with Theo Wilson

Theo Wilson spent 20 years in the U.S. Coast Guard before transitioning to cross-cultural mission work. Originally from the U.S. he has been serving in South East Asia for nine years, the last three years as a team leader.

Dear Friend,

I am grateful for this opportunity to write to you and share some thoughts I've had on the leadership of a cross-cultural ministry team.

The worst 'leaders' are afraid of being replaced someday. When I served in the Coast Guard we always talked about 'training our relief' (the person who would take our position some day). We should always be developing the next generation of leaders with great enthusiasm. It's like the first time one of my sons beat me in arm wrestling. It wasn't a time of regret (ok, maybe a little). No, this was my son! Rejoice in the development and success of our teammates!

My wife used to tell me, "It is more important to be godly than to be right." (I'm a little slow, but I finally understood that it has nothing to do with actually being right, but rather my insisting that others agree with me that I'm right.) Each day ask the Holy Spirit to apply the Word from your devotions to your life first, then to those closest to you. Then ask Him to apply it to each of your teammates' lives.

Be a student of your teammates. Let them lead in areas of their strengths while letting them develop in weaker areas with the help of someone else, if necessary (it doesn't have to be you). Never be afraid to say, "That's a great idea you have! Let's do that!"

Sometimes you just need to let people try and fail at something (as long as the consequences are not too devastating) so that they learn for themselves what you've already tried to communicate. Experience leaves a more indelible impression than I do.

Oftentimes people think their leaders don't communicate enough; therefore, it's better to try to over-communicate what is going on.

Learn to be a great follower.

Best,
Theo Wilson

Lunch with Elliot

Elliot Josiah Park, a Korean-American, had many years of pastoral experience in America before moving to the mission field of the Middle East 7 years ago. He has been leading a mission team there for the last five years as well as serving in church leadership.

Dear New Leader,

An extremely helpful phrase for me as a mission team leader has been 'appropriate confidence'. I first encountered this term in a card my wife had given me soon after we started getting to know each other. Even at that point, she recognized my lack of self-confidence and offered a step to recovery you won't read in a typical self-help book. Appropriate confidence is different than self-confidence. It's more like God-confidence. It is not confidence in one's own leadership abilities – experience, charisma, or hard work – it is confidence in knowing that God has placed you by His divine authority and providence as a leader in whatever position you are in and therefore He's going to use you …warts, mistakes, strengths, gifts, and all. For all of us in leadership, may our lives be marked by appropriate confidence.

I believe that being on a mission team should be like doing missions. In other words, the way people relate to others on a mission team should be the same way they approach missions. From my experience, this is usually not the case. For example, we've known British and Australian missionaries who have struggled more with Americans on their team than with locals. Perhaps this is because with locals, we expect there to be differences in culture and worldview and thus we are more prepared for those differences. With some of our team members, we may speak the same language and may both come from the West, so we are less prepared (and more surprised) when we encounter differences in culture or mind-set.

My wife and I have encountered this phenomenon personally in Pioneers and in our contact with other mission agencies. Before moving to the mission field, our spiritual experience was shaped for well over thirty years in the sub-culture of Asian-American Christianity. This profoundly molded the way we pray, the way we share, and the way we view God, the Bible, and each other.

As an example, organizational prayer times tend to be stressful, pressure-filled, and draining times for me. The simple reason is that in general, people pray in a way that's different than the way I'm used to; I'm used to everyone praying out loud all at once ('Korean style') versus one at a time while everyone else listens and agrees. Should I adjust and learn to pray like most people in our organization do? Sure, that's what missionaries are supposed to do – adapt. It is what I've done, and I expect that one day I will be comfortable with it. But my question is this: how much do others adjust the way they're used to praying?

Another example can be seen in the way that we share how things are going with others. The best way to describe it is that when we share the way we're accustomed to sharing, people often feel sorry for us. There are a number of times my wife and I have shared and the "tsk-tsk" in response was almost audible. As a bit of background, Asian-American culture is similar to Asian culture in its introspective tendencies, and we tend to share in a very self-deprecating manner. At the Asian-American church we attended for years, it was common to hear people share things such as: "I'm really proud," "I need to repent about such and such," "I'm so selfish." This type of sharing is encouraged; it's considered life-giving and a blessing. It is this way because at our church we embrace the idea that grace is most appreciated in the backdrop of sin. When one's sin is highlighted, then God's love, grace, and redemption are highlighted that much more. It can also be explained by the influence of Asian culture, where people are expected to focus on negative aspects of themselves and allow others to lift them up. To speak confidently is generally considered proud, shameful, and wrong. A common biblical example upheld as a deep encouragement at our church is found in 1 Timothy 1:15-16, where Paul calls himself, in the present tense near the end of his life, the worst of sinners.

The point of all this is not a call to revolutionize the style of prayer or sharing in our organization. Rather, it is to highlight the fact that we often assume – without realizing it – that our way of doing things is the only way (or right way). Or at times we aren't aware of or haven't encountered other ways of doing things and thus don't consider doing things any other way. In either case, the ensuing assumption is that everyone else should do it our way, which intended or not, places the responsibility on other people to adjust. If my wife and I feel so strongly this pressure to conform, as leaders no less, what must it be like for others on a team who come from a different culture (or sub-culture of Christianity)? Will they also feel this unspoken pressure to conform to the leaders' way of doing Christianity?

This is not only applicable to the issue of globalization within mission teams, but it also has a bearing on missiology. Are we assuming that our sub-culture of Christianity is the only one or the right one? (I'm writing to all missionaries regardless of culture of origin, because we all have our own culture.) The people we're reaching may be in the cultural majority, but once they are in our group or under our leadership, effectively they are in the minority. And if we are not extremely careful, they will conform as well. We may end up not planting churches, but rather transplanting churches marked by our culture.

Again, my wife and I aren't exempt from falling into this trap because we are from American minorities. We're incredibly gifted at making incorrect assumptions. One team member who eventually returned home prematurely struggled almost from the first moment she arrived. We tried to reach out to her, encourage her, be available, and listen as best as we could. We discovered from some other team members that she was extremely offended and hurt by our conversations. After several not-so-easy follow-up discussions we realized that we had made the huge and incorrect assumption that she, like us, was working from a framework of total depravity and repentance. In other words, we believe there is always a repentance issue in every situation, and identifying that issue is paramount to going through the situation in a spiritually healthy manner. She didn't have a similar view of repentance, and our assumption that she did led to a great deal of misunderstanding. That assumption springs from our sub-culture of Christianity.

My advice? Be a learner always. Try not to assume. Ask lots of questions. Give opportunities to those from other cultures (or sub-cultures of Christianity) to lead. And give them the freedom, openly, to lead in a way they are comfortable with. Empower them by saying, "I'd love for you to lead the worship or the prayer time. And lead the way you feel comfortable leading. Even if people don't respond the way you expect, keep at it. We're all learning together." And then create opportunities to discuss some of the differences and feelings people have about them.

I do hope this letter results in more open dialogue and more of an awareness of how much our culture influences us in ways we don't even realize. In turn, it is my hope that Pioneers (and all mission organizations) might be an increasingly internationalized with a growing effectiveness in seeing Scripturally-sound, culturally relevant, truly indigenous churches being planted (and church planting movements started) in the most unreached places in the world.

Grace,
Elliot

Week 3

Day 19

Coffee break with Jonathan

Jonathan Hankin was a business leader for 10 years in America before moving to the Middle East 10 years ago. Over the last nine years Jonathan has been involved in team and field mission leadership.

Dear New Leaders,

As you begin your new leadership role I want to encourage you that this role you're are taking on is ordained by God Himself. He has chosen you for this time and for this purpose for reasons that seem obvious but also for reasons that may not be as obvious. The obvious reasons are listed out in your organization's handbook and team leader role description, and relate to the responsibilities you have taken on. The not so obvious reasons I would like to discuss below.

As you embark on this leadership position, I am reminded and want to remind you that the reason God has put you in this position is foremost because He wants to have a closer relationship with you. Yes, you want to lead well, help form new teams, motivate your people, plan events, and do all that is involved in being a leader, but that is all secondary. I do hope all those things happen. I believe they will and you will do a great job at them, but that is not your primary calling. Your primary calling as a leader is to be led by God and to depend on Him so much that He will guide you in all you do. Out of that will then be fruit that is from God and will sustain itself instead of you trying to sustain it by your efforts.

Because God wants a closer relationship with you, He will use this leadership time to prune you so that you will bear much fruit. He will humble you in ways you could not see coming and will cause you to depend on Him more and more. Satan will also try to get you to focus on your skills and expertise instead of on God in order to make you less fruitful. Think about it this way: when you get to Heaven and God welcomes you in, and you get to see the fruit you were part of, you don't want to hear, "Good job my faithful servant, you did well leading my people and I used them for My Glory; but I really wanted to know you more and to use you more because I love you. You did well, but I really wished you had spent more time with Me instead of leaning on your own understanding; leadership would have been an easier burden and you would have had more joy."

I am sure there is more I could write but if you can keep this personal focus on your relationship with God the center of your leadership I believe the rest will fall into place.

Standing together,
Jonathan

Lunch with Yung

*Y*ung Wai Lap has served many places during his 17 years on the field. Originally from Hong Kong, his missionary career has taken him to Africa, Asia and South America. For the last 10 years, he has had the privilege to serve in various leadership roles in Asia.

Dear Leader,

After serving Him for some time as part of different combinations of teams in different parts of the world, I am convinced that team leaders play a significant role in building up a strong team that can powerfully and effectively serve the Lord, as well as preventing hurt and separation within the team. Apart from constantly praying for individual teammates, here are some tips for new team leaders, to avoid hurts and splits and to instead build up teammates to serve the Lord in unity and spirit:

A team leader needs to be aware of one's own character and personality; this is crucial to avoid team conflict. Many team conflicts and most serious conflicts usually come from character clash instead of other so-called team conflicts or other apparently legitimate causes. Many leaders do have strong characters – inside, outside, or both. Their character easily clashes with those team members who also have strong characters and personalities. Some team members choose to argue or even fight with each other, which damages team unity and causes discord or division. Some team members choose to keep silent until the point they cannot bear any more, and then choose to leave the team. Many will not share the true reason they have decided to leave the team until they take the action to leave. The most extreme case I know is that the team member left the team to go back to their home country without telling the team leader and team. The team leader also needs to be aware of the character and personality of each team member so that they can help prevent team members from crashing into each other. The team leader has the responsibility to be aware of the character and personalities of different team members in order to better nurture team spirit and build up team unity, and avoid team conflict.

Our company is getting more and more internationalized; many teams do have members with different cultural background of different countries; e.g., my team has Caucasian Americans, American Chinese, American Hong Kong, Singaporean and Hong Kong people. A team leader needs to learn and study the culture of team members so they can understand where they are coming from and make communication easier and clearer with minimal misunderstanding. Misunderstanding one's meaning comes from miscommunication; miscommunication with each other comes from being unable to understand where they are coming from. Leaders must not expect team members to have the same way of thinking and worldview as him/her. In general, western, especially US, culture is more dominant in a team when the team has non-western members. Non-western members are in the minority in many teams; leaders, especially those who do not have cross-cultural team experience, need to put in extra effort to understand the diversity of different cultural backgrounds and worldviews of each member that can balance the team dynamic and harmonize relationship among the team.

Leaders need to pay attention to the individual needs of members. The leader plays the role of facilitator to support and help members to learn and serve effectively in a cross-cultural setting. Paying attention appropriately to individual needs of each member is one of the best ways to minimize the tension in the team due to the stress, anxiety and constant worry of individual members. Of course, the leader should not expect himself/herself to fulfil all the needs of individual members. Leaders can always refer members to meet with the right personnel for their needs fulfilment, such as organizational member care, professional counsellor, spiritual mentor, coach, etc. The more needs are fulfilled; the more the members can focus on ministries and team life. On the other hand, leaders also need to be aware of the gender issue among members; the leader should avoid paying too much attention to opposite sex single members, in order to avoid misunderstanding and temptation between the team leader and team member. It is always wise to get help from the appropriate person who has the same gender as the member who is in need.

We may tend to think we are the same if all leaders and members come from the same country. Even if they do come from the same country, cultural background, language background, etc., each single individual is still different and unique in many ways. Leaders should be aware of the differences between individuals and avoid 'we' and 'they' in the team, no matter whether the team has members coming from one region of the same country, or more than one nationality of different countries. The 'we' and 'they' idea does undermine the bonding and unity of the team.

Many conflicts do not come from the content of disagreements or arguments. Instead, many conflicts come from the attitudes of the people who speak. Our tone, voice, gesture and the way of expression do reflect our attitude inside our hearts; do we want to make things happen, move things forward and build up life …or to prove ourselves, fight back or destroy life? The ways of expression can carry more meaning than the content of words, or even change the meaning of words. Leaders not only need to be aware his/her attitude, but also the members' attitude when communicating with each other. One of the best ways to avoid or minimize conflicts that arise due to attitude problems is to take the course of inter-personal communication skill.

The personal vision of its leader does not necessarily need to be the team vision for all members. It is important to get input from members before finalizing the vision for the whole team. Usually, the leader is the first one who forms the initial vision, but it is good to include members to sharpen a clear vision for the whole team that can establish ownership of vision.

Leaders should nurture an open atmosphere in the team for members to honestly and sincerely share their views, understandings, struggles, feelings and hearts with other members. The more room and space the leader creates for teammates to share what's in their heart, the stronger bonding and unity will be built up in the team. Once misunderstanding happens, it will be the chance for Satan to work among the team. Open and honest sharing not only can develop good understanding and harmony of practically working together and supporting each other, but also avoid gossiping, which is a powerful tool of our enemy to break the team down.

It is easy to be a humble learner when we are new to live and work in cross-cultural setting. Many are ready to go to the field with learning mode in the first few years when there is so much to learn. It is harder to be a humble servant after learning some cultures, customs and traditions of field, as well as being able to master the local language or dialect to communicate with local people. We tend to serve the Lord with our own effort, own ways and own resources (usually from back home). We feel more confident in ourselves or even proud of ourselves after we make some achievements. It is a completely different level of humility to be a humble leader; it is hard to keep a humble attitude when we are appointed to be a leader and given authority. When our senior leadership approve and appoint us to be a leader, the fact is they have confidence in us and see we are able and suitable to lead a team. Leaders must keep watching his/her heart and attitude from time to time; keep humbling oneself to serve for His glory.

Certainly, the roles and responsibilities of leaders and team members are different. However, being appointed to be leader does not necessarily mean he/she is better and wiser than the team. The difference is that the leader walks few or ten steps ahead of the members in field setting. Both serve the Most High on the same foundation of His grace and mercy. The leader indeed should keep humbling himself/herself to learn and journey with his team together as they serve together in the same body of Christ.

Blessings,
Yung

WEEK 3

DAY 20

Coffee break with Marcus

Marcus Ferreira left his home in Brazil for Central Asia 10 years ago. Marcus assumed leadership of a mission team three years ago.

Dear New Missionary Leader,

I have so many things to say to you before you arrive on the field and become a new team leader.

First of all, you were invited to be part of an amazing project. You were invited to be part of God's mission. Therefore, before you arrive here, you need to understand that it is not really your mission. God was, God is, and always will be in charge of His project.

I know that you have so many ideas, so many projects in your mind, but I advise you to arrive with a humble and teachable heart. This attitude will help you not only with your teammates but also in the whole process of learning the language and the culture of the people God sent you to serve.

Talking about language, I advise you to spend at least one year focusing on language learning. Be intentional in being with locals. Connection with a small group or a local church is fundamental to helping you thrive. It is very important that you minimize your time with foreigners. I know that in the beginning it will be hard, but this will help you speak their language faster and better.

Another thing I want you to keep in your mind is that in your first year, sometimes longer, you will feel useless. You will come to the field to work, to serve, and to lead; but in your first years, your main goal will be to learn the language and culture and build relationships. Maybe there will be people demanding 'results'. Maybe you will demand results of yourself, but remember that these first years will be crucial for your future ministry.

Ah! Before I forget, do not be afraid to be part of and lead a multicultural team. I know it seems frightening, but it will be worth it. When you figure out how to deal with these different cultures, you will see how great and rich it is to serve and lead a team with different worldviews. You will learn to see the multiple facets of God's grace and wisdom in each one of them.

In Him,
Marcus

Week 3 : Day 20 :

Lunch with Chris

Chris Carey has been serving in East Asia for more than eight years. For nearly all of that time he has also been leading a team.

Dear New Leader,

I've been a team leader for almost eight years now. If I could sit down with my much younger self right now, I'd tell him not to forget five key things, and I'd like to share those same things with you.

First, don't forget your family. Paul, sharing with Timothy about what kind of man God has in mind to lead His church, spends the most time talking about managing his household well. (See 1 Timothy 3:4-5.) Why is managing your household important? Managing one's family life translates directly to managing the household of God.

Mission teams are no exception (and we can so easily forget this). Forgetting your family, not caring for them spiritually, not seeking their good, selfishly neglecting them (and often calling it a 'sacrifice') for the sake of your ministry, is a quick way to a lot pain and burnout and likely even worse. Managing your household well equips, empowers, and qualifies you to manage other ministry responsibilities well.

Don't forget your family.

Second, don't forget your Christian heritage. Although Christianity has been around a long time, for some reason, missionaries like to come overseas and brush aside thousands of years of biblical and wise patterns of church functioning. I observe countless missionaries who view attending church as 'optional', the commissioning of qualified church leadership in new church plants as something to do away with (because it slows down the 'movement'), and the Bible as the authoritative Word of God something to be supplanted by other literature – or even their own thoughts or practical experience.

Beware, leader! Beware leaving behind thousands of years of wisdom for fleeting and passing 'missionary methods'! Beware redefining that which has transformed lives and peoples and nations and cultures for centuries past!

Don't forget your Christian heritage.

Third, don't forget that Jesus unifies. In The Pursuit of God, A.W. Tozer paints a beautiful picture of how unity happens. Imagine a room filled with pianos, all out of tune. Then imagine someone tuning the first piano, then going to the next piano and tuning that piano to the first one, the next piano to that one, and so on. What do you get at the end? A room filled with out of tune pianos.

Imagine the scene again, but this time the piano tuner pulls out a tuning fork. One by one, the piano tuner tunes each piano to the tuning fork, to the standard. What do you have at the end? A room filled with pianos, all in tune.

So it is with Christ. He is our standard and to Him we must look (be 'in tune')! So much time and energy can be spent trying to unify your team (social gatherings, discussions, meetings, retreats…) and these things have their place and value; but this most-essential, foundational principle cannot be forgotten: turn your (spiritual) eyes and the eyes of your team to Jesus!

'Turn your eyes upon Jesus!
Look full in His wonderful face.
And the things of earth will grow strangely dim.
In the light of His glory and grace.
Don't forget that Jesus unifies.'

Fourth, don't forget your God. This is something you already know. Walking closely with God is the most important thing you can do while you're overseas. He is your strength, your life, your Help, your Hope and if you do not continue in deep intimacy with Him, you lose sight of it all. Like a plant without sun, you will shrivel.

The shocking thing is not this truth; it's that knowing this truth, you will quickly forget it. The busyness of life, family, ministry, platform, and on and on will come and take your eyes off the One you went to serve. In no time at all, what originally was about Him and borne of our knowing Him, becomes all about you.

He is your Source. As one of Hudson Taylor's favourite hymns says:

'Jesus I am resting, resting.
In the joy of what Thou art
I am finding out the greatness
Of Thy loving heart.
Don't forget your God.'

Finally, don't forget that Jesus loves you. Sometimes I call this 'kindergarten Christianity'; it's so simple, so fundamental that kids sing about it in Sunday School.

But it's all too often forgotten. I forgot it.

The Apostle Paul, talking about the new life in Christ says, "I have been crucified with Christ and I no longer live, but Christ lives in me. The life I now live in the body, I live by faith in the Son of God, who loved me and gave himself for me" (Galatians 2:20.)

"Who loved me and gave himself for me." Just think of that: Jesus truly loves you! That's worth a lifetime of meditation on that phrase alone. He loved you before you even trusted Him, while His enemy. He loved you before you ever 'did' something for the kingdom. And He loves you now – no matter what you 'do for Him' or not. What amazing grace… Every day – through His Word, prayer and meditation, by the power of the Holy Spirit – press this truth deep in your soul.

Don't forget that Jesus loves you.

Much grace to you in your own leadership journey,
Chris

Day 21

Day of Reflection…

Take a moment to reflect on the 'conversations' of the last 6 days…

- *What portions of the letters did you underline? What struck you or jumped out at you?*

- *Is there anything you disagreed with or would like to have further discussion about?*

- *What themes seem to be standing out to you? How do these things tie together?*

- *Sit for a few minutes and ask the Lord, What would you have me walk away with and take to heart or implement? With whom would you have me discuss this?*

Week Four

Week 4

Day 22

Coffee break with Taylor and Katarina

Taylor and Katarina Shead grew up in America and Australia respectively, and met on the field in East Asia in 2004, where they accepted the responsibility of team leadership four years ago.

Dear Servant of the Gospel,

Thank you for being willing to bless the church with the gifts and wisdom God has blessed you with. Thank you for being willing to be the instrument God uses to stretch others under your care. Like Paul, "I keep asking that the God of our Lord Jesus Christ, the glorious Father, may give you the Spirit of wisdom and revelation, so that you may know him better. I pray that the eyes of your heart may be enlightened in order that you may know the hope to which he has called you…" (Ephesians 1:17-18a.)

We tend to believe that our work for God springs from and is fuelled by our knowledge of God, but we don't always live that way. We know that we don't, and we have learned that just having a calling or a passion is no substitute for having the hope of His calling. Every day has troubles of its own, Jesus assured us. But every day that starts with a hearty, "Not my will, but Thy will be done," is a day that is filled with hope.

A mind that has been enlightened by God is a mind that knows the hope of His calling. That mind is always found attached to a body that is experienced in prayer. Not just praying through Operation World, or the team strategy document. By all means, do that. But pray for and with your spouse and children, if you have them, like their happiness depended on it. Because it does.

Pray for your unconverted friends and neighbours like their rescue from hell depends on it. What you do in secret is the very essence of love. Pray for your team members whenever their faces come to mind. Even if it's 3:00 in the morning. Especially if you want to quit because of them.

We are still learning just how much of the battle we fight against the powers happens before we even feel the need to pray. When our thoughts finally turn Godward, we know with absolute certainty that He is always more loving and more merciful and more able than we think He is. His outstretched arms are still mighty to save you not only from death, but also from sin, shame, fear, and failure.

As you pray, never forget that your shoulders are pressed up against sisters and brothers who have communed with God before you. Beware of any sentence that starts with, "You've heard that it was said, but..." unless you happen to be reading the Gospel of Matthew. Remember that God has blessed you with the church rather than the other way around. Read old books and listen to old saints. Work quietly to earn a reputation as a man or woman who loves God, the church, and who's been mastered by the Scriptures. We can't think of a better gift you can give your family, your team, or your host community than that.

Finally, remember the words of the Lord. The one who's been forgiven much, loves much.

Peace,
Taylor and *Katarina*

Lunch with August

August Kuehn, born and raised in America, has spent the last 15 years focused on ministry to the Muslim world. August's journey has taken him to four different countries and cultures and in the last 10 years has led him into leadership as well.

Dear New Leader,

I would certainly not consider myself to be a great leader. I appreciate the opportunity to serve as one, but I suspect there are others that do a far better job and are more skilled and equipped than me. However, in my ten plus years of leading cross-cultural teams, I have learned some important lessons, many of them through heartbreak and disappointment. Yet I feel these lessons are making me into a better leader with each passing season.

Be a reluctant leader. I used to think that leadership was something to which I should aspire. I thought it was the Christian world's equivalent of getting a promotion or being recognized for a job well done. When given a new title or new role, it felt like a pat on the back. But I soon began to realize that this aspiration is often rooted in pride and a desire for attention and recognition. I have witnessed others in this work jockey for a title in the organization and then become devastated when they didn't get it. In some cases, this disappointment led to leaving the field all together.

I remember one conversation with a leader of mine and I told him that I was not interested in submitting my name for a leadership role that had wider responsibility. I told him I did not aspire to 'moving up' in the organization. "That's the very thing that now makes you an interesting candidate," he replied. I was not asked to take that new role and was very content with the decision.

When I think of leadership roles, I'm often reminded of Jesus' words, "When someone invites you to a wedding feast, do not take the place of honor, for a person more distinguished than you may have been invited. If so, the host who invited both of you will come and say to you, 'Give this person your seat.' Then, humiliated, you will have to take the least important place. But when you are invited, take the lowest place, so that when your host comes, he will say to you, 'Friend, move up to a better place.' Then you will be honored in the presence of all the other guests. For all those who exalt themselves will be humbled, and those who humble themselves will be exalted" (Luke 14:8-11.)

I'm certainly not implying that being in leadership is a bad thing. Rather, I've learned that we need to check our motives and seek first the Kingdom of God and His purposes in us and around us. Rather than aspire to a role, title, or position, we must aspire to reflect God's glory in all we do and trust Him to bring that about in the best possible way for each of us.

"Leader" is a life, not a title. In my early years of leadership, I would read Hebrews 13:17, "Have confidence in your leaders and submit to their authority, because they keep watch over you as those who must give an account. Do this so that their work will be a joy, not a burden, for that would be of no benefit to you." I mistakenly believed that having a title after my name granted me special authority and privilege. Instead, experience began to demonstrate that the only thing the title of "Leader" awarded me was a big target on my back at which exceeding numbers of complaints, insults, and unreasonable expectations were hurled.

True leadership is a measure of influence. Influence is exerted and well received in the context of a mutually caring, trusting, and sacrificial relationship. I soon discovered that in order to be a better leader I needed to become a better follower of Christ. I needed to become a kinder, gentler person. I needed to live a life that others considered trustworthy of following rather than seeking to wield influence (or, God forbid, power) over those entrusted to my care. In essence, I seek to become more like the person I would be pleased to follow.

A leader does more listening than speaking. Often when we see leaders in the media they are politicians or military figures or sports coaches who are giving rousing inspirational talks or waxing eloquently about their vision or strategy. This can tempt us to believe that the best thing a leader has to offer is what pours from the mouth. However, I am continually confronted with the reality that I don't know as much as I think I know. The best chance I have at leading is if I am listening as much or more than I'm speaking.

Unless I consciously create time and space to be still and listen to what the Lord would want to say to me, what He would speak into any and every situation, I risk leading from my own wisdom. I risk missing His perfect timing and I miss out on His best. Furthermore, those with whom I work will be much more confident following a leader who is listening to God and leading from that place than a leader who is irregular or inconsistent in seeking wisdom from above.

In addition, a leader must spend ample time listening to and inquiring of those he or she leads. Politicians are often accused of being out of touch with their constituents. How much more important is it for us as leaders of God's teams to develop good communication and a relationship of mutual respect with those we lead. As James exhorts us we must, "be quick to hear, slow to speak, slow to anger…" (James 1:19.)

Humbly submit to God's transforming work. Just about everything I've mentioned thus far can be summarized by one word: humility. As leaders we must walk in humility before our God and before those we serve. In my relatively short time in service, I've seen leaders tumble and fall. I've seen some tremendous Kingdom work displayed only to be tarnished by a leader that ultimately stopped submitting to God's works and ways. I myself have come near the edge of burnout in service thinking that my ways were better than His ways.

As we become humble, transformed leaders in our cross-cultural work, we will have some fantastic opportunities to be a blessing to many, to shine light into darkness, and to be the hands and feet of our Saviour in some of the world's darkest places.

I was recently praying again about this transforming work of the Spirit in my own life, asking God to continue to grant me humility and help me to submit to His ways. As I prayed, God gave me a picture of a little child learning to ride a bike. Seated on the bike, the child was propelled down the street by his father's strong hand firmly gripping the seat from behind. The father's hand provided power, stability, guidance, and protection. However, the child, as courage and competence increased, began to wave off the father's hand: "Let go! I'm fine. I don't need your help anymore."

It's true. The child can learn to be a competent bike rider apart from his father's hand. But God's desire for us as leaders is not to become competent to the point we seek autonomy and independence. Rather, He desires that we keep pace with Him. He invites us to move in His power. He longs for us to respond to His guidance and go forth in the confidence of His protection and provision.

I guess I'm still learning how to ride this bike well, but I'm thankful for these and many other lessons I've learned along the way that are shaping me into the kind of leader God might be pleased to use for His glory.

Blessings,
August

Week 4
Day 23

Coffee break with Mark

Mark Newham answered God's call to mission when he moved from England to Mongolia 22 years ago. During the last 22 years he has served in many ways, including 14 years as a team leader.

Dear Leader,

There are so many different types of leaders, ranging from those who are very structured and gather a team around them to fulfil a cooperate vision, to those who have no defined purpose for their team but see their responsibility as enabling others to fulfil their personal vision. Wherever we fall within the spectrum of this definition I believe we each have responsibilities to contemplate as we lead others.

Firstly, I believe we should take the responsibility of leading with seriousness. The Anglican liturgy that forms part of the marriage service advises husbands and wives, as they enter into the covenant of marriage, that they should not do so lightly or selfishly, but reverently and responsibly in the sight of Almighty God. This may sound a little too heavy to be applied to a team context but I believe God brings people and asks us to lead with a reverent fear and responsibly. He asks us to commit ourselves to leading others in a prayerful, godly manner.

What does leading in a godly manner entail?

For me one of the keys is being willing to serve those we lead. I love John's example of Jesus as a servant in chapter 13 of his gospel. As we know well, Jesus got down on his hands and knees and did the grubbiest job possible for his disciples. He washed their feet which had tramped through the dust and grim of the city streets. God calls us too to wash, to serve, and enable others; and at times this requires that we kneel and lay down our own desires and vision in order to enable others. It is not about us trying to 'climb the greasy pole', as the English say, rather it is about us holding the ladder steady while those we lead scale the wall before them.

In seeking to serve and enable others I also believe we should maximise opportunities to grow and mature those who are part of our team or are within our sphere of influence. Naturally, each of us must have a commitment to personal growth and maturing in Christ first, but in our leadership role we should also actively plan and present opportunities to allow others to exercise their gifts freely. We need to nurture and challenge, as well as allow for the development of the gifts God has placed in the lives of our team members and friends. Our team members need to be able to exercise their gifts within the safety and security of our team as well as within the ministry settings God provides.

Personally, this is the area I have derived most pleasure and satisfaction from as a leader. Watching team members and others God has given into my care grow and go on to fulfil the ministry they believe God has given to them fills me with a longing to keep growing and serving myself. And I trust and pray that you will know this deepening joy too.

Blessings,
Mark

Lunch with MYL

M. Y. L. Elggin left his native New Zealand 10 years ago for China. Just over nine years ago, he assumed the role of team leader for his mission team.

Dear New Leader,

As you embark on your leadership journey, I'm imagining what I would say to myself at the outset of my own. Perhaps these thoughts directed at my younger self will be an encouragement for you…

If only you had known. Over the next ten years you will face multiple medical evacuations, demons, hidden marital failure, secrets that tear your team apart, scheming, insults, and accusations. You will be lied to, feared, and even hated. You will feel bone-achingly tired. You will sit up in the night wondering if it is all worth it. You will grieve over people who will be forced to leave. You will feel isolated and lonely. You will have to face your own shortcomings and fears. You will have to face yourself.

But don't harden your heart. Use 'Sonscreen'!

You will have high hopes starting out. You are going to have the best team ever. Finally there is an opportunity to lead things the way they should be led. The only problem is that there are so many things that are out of your control. The theory of what you are trying to do and the real world reality of what you are going to face are seemingly worlds apart. Learning about cultural stress and team conflict are different to living it. Change is your best and worst friend.

You are going to hurt and get hurt. People will reject you, your advice, and your guidance. The devouring lion will eat his fill. He will certainly try. Don't underestimate the battle your team is in. Evaluate to learn from your mistakes and to learn the enemy's attacks. Patterns will emerge. Know that before anything good happens there will be attacks. Know that afterward the attacks will increase, not simply dissipate. Expect it to be hard and dirty. You have skin in the game and it's going to cost.

This is not a drone war. You are not a general. Expect to need the field hospital. Expect everyone to be a medic and first responder. Your teammates are going to phone you when their children are screaming as they see demons climbing the walls of their rooms. Your teammates are going to fight over silly things as the pressure builds. Your children are going to get really sick. You will spend hours in foreign hospitals. Expect your and your teammates' marriages to be under attack. Your singles will battle loneliness. You are all on the front lines. It's going to be way messier than you think. Expect to get hurt.

The first mistake you will make is to want everyone to like you. You need to learn that you are not here to be liked but to lead. Ask the hard questions. Keep asking the hard questions. Leading always comes at a personal cost. People will not like you asking the hard questions.

The second mistake you will make is to be overly optimistic and think others are willing to be led …or actually see you as a leader. You will learn that people will say all sorts of things to make it to the field.

The third mistake you will make is to think that everyone knows what working on a team together means. We are surprisingly independent and don't like sacrificing what we want to do for the sake of others.

The fourth mistake you will make is to want everyone to like you. Did I mention that change is difficult?

You will be tempted to defend yourself in a time of deep personal attack. Take a few deep breaths, listen to your co-leader wife, and trust in God. Don't be afraid of becoming someone's scapegoat.

Many a foe is overcome by choosing the less-travelled path of grace and peace. It will mean humiliation and defeat, but it will lead to victory. I think there is something in the Bible about that.

You will find the key to team leading is praying. Pray a lot and then pray some more. Yes, you need to be faithful to do the practical stuff like team meetings, casting vision, holding people accountable to vision, having up-to-date crisis documentation, guiding and mentoring people. Team management sets the game in play. Prayer is the game changer. Praying and helping people to pray will be the thing that opens doors and hearts. Don't give up hope and don't give up praying. You will need to pray for the same thing for years. Also don't forget to get everyone to pack an emergency 'go bag' and have their insurance details handy, preferably have them stuck on the side of the fridge.

There will be periods of immense joy. You will grow. You will come to see that working overseas intimately reflects the Incarnation. You and your teammates will move from positions of power to powerlessness. You all will have the gift of becoming like children again. You will learn to walk, eat, and speak in a new culture and language. You and your team will have the joy of entering into a more personally intimate relationship with your Creator. It is traumatic, but there is a deeply satisfying outcome to be achieved. Yes, you will know the joy of, and be able to rejoice with angels over, a new name written in the book of life. Your vision of who God is and what He is doing will explode as you see God's face reflected in your team. More importantly, however, is that God will finally be able to mould you into what you were always meant to be.

Don't give up. Don't forget to use 'Sonscreen'!

Blessings,
MYL

Week 4
Day 24

Coffee break with Francis

Francis Avoyi, originally from Togo, has been serving in the field of West Africa for 18 years, 10 years in team leadership, and the last seven years as the field leader for that area.

Dear New Leader,

Below are a few thoughts for you as you move ahead in leading a team. You may choose to disregard these points, but for me these ones kept me for over the past years in my role as a leader. We are not leaders until we have followers. So as Christian leaders, we need to invest our time, energy, and resources in the people we are leading. We can do so in the following ways:

Know their condition. Each person will like to know that he is important and as leaders we need to value them, check on them regularly, and see them not only in the working environment, but in real life what they are going through. A leader can only lead the people he knows. Focusing only on the work and not on the people who are working is less productive. It is important to make them have the heart for what they do, so there is need to care for them as a shepherd cares for his sheep.

Help them identify with you. How will you feel when you know that your leader identifies himself with you? We need to be authentic and trustworthy in dealing with the people we lead.

Create a safe environment for your team. Each teammate waking up in the morning will want to be in a safe environment. A leader needs to eliminate the uncertainty that distracts his people. They need to be well informed by you first, either bad or good news, before they hear it from other sources. When they feel confident that you will let them know as soon as possible, they will be less susceptible to the rumour mill. When they cannot trust a leader to keep them up to date about matters that affect them, a piece of bad news will flame them up.

Have the heart of a shepherd. Great leadership is a lifestyle and not a technique; people don't care about how much you know until they know how much you care. It is important on a daily basis to decide who pays the price. If in the course of accomplishing their duty there is a challenge or difficulties, they would want to know if you are there for them, to take the first blow. Leading the people after the heart of a shepherd will make them follow. Leadership comes at a price that few are willing to pay.

I hope these few thoughts will help keep you going on this journey with our Lord Jesus.

Till I hear from you my brother, remain blessed,
Francis

Week 4: Day 24:

Lunch with Willow

Willow Song is a dual national of New Zealand and Taiwan. She has spent the last 10 years living and working in China, the last nine of those as a team leader.

Dear New Leader,

So you have become a team leader. Does it feel exciting or daunting? I hope you don't mind me sharing with you my two cents' worth. What I'm about to say are the many mistakes or near compromises that I have learnt along the way. When I first received the responsibility, I was scared; I was worried. I was looking at it all wrong. My vision was too small for God, and I was too naïve to be useful. I know that if you are anything like me, you may not fully understand what I am going to say below, but in time I hope that some of what I am about to communicate will make sense and I hope you will find some encouragement or direction from them when the opportunities presents itself.

Team is worth it! To build a good team is not at all about efficiency or productivity. It is more about learning how to love each other the right way, how to care for the weakest in the team, and to learn how to have unity with Christ (not you) as the head. It takes a lot of effort and energy, in fact more than if one goes it alone. But the biggest reason for team is that we are going about planting a community – churches – in places where there is no existing community like it. How will people understand what that type of community looks like, if they have not seen it modelled in us first?

Some may think that, because they are unable to openly admit to others about their association in a closed country, how we treat each other in teams is not important. This is not the case. In a closed country, precisely because people are not free to say exactly what they mean, they watch other's actions more closely than in a culture that is more open. People learn, and they sense the relationship between us. They observe what we say about each other, and they see the actions we perform for each other.

Hence, the kind of community – team – you create is going to affect the community you want to plant – the local church. We are not planting individuals, we are planting communities. What kind of leadership do you display to your team? What kind of atmosphere do you value in your team? What kind of people are in your team and how do you treat each other? Do you value some people more than others? How do you decide things? How do you together seek the Father? More often than not, the locals you interact with will reflect back like a mirror, not only the spirituality of the individuals, but also the health of the community.

Sometimes we see division between different people within the local Church – the age-old conflict between different people with different backgrounds. It was there at the time with Jesus and later with Paul. It's certainly here in our time. Our team should display the answer to these questions. Should I still try to love and worship with someone who is very different from me? What does it mean to care for the weakest of the body parts and how is God glorified through that? Should I forgive my brothers and sisters; and how do we resolve conflicts?

It is, therefore, important to accept people onto your team who are different from you, see them as part of your ministry to understand, walk alongside, and love them – be it differences in outlook, background, cultures, personalities, even theology. If we can love and work with each other despite the differences, this sends an example to the people around us of what a Christ-centred community looks like. If we can shine out that our only commonality is Christ and our love for Him – not being 'Western', American, 'wealthy,' 'coffee drinkers'

– then it lessens the possible baggage this Good News will bear. There is less chance of it being tainted by masks that are not intended to be associated with the Gospel.

Team is worth it; it's hard and to build it well takes a lot of effort, but if you short-change team, you may see the community you are trying to reach do the same. If their leadership cannot work with each other, if they do not know how to listen to the Spirit together, you may find that the health of this group will struggle for a long time.

You don't have to 'like' someone to have them be part of the team, but you do have to care for them and love them to lead them. There are a lot of assumptions made when teammates meet for the first time. We all have our differences. We need time to really listen to each other and to love each other. It is not only for the purpose of working with each other or getting what we need from each other. Teammates are part of everyone's responsibility and ministry. Our effort is not merely towards the locals. If we cannot understand and love each other, how do we love and understand our host country?

The biggest misconception about team is that we need to be best buddies and have the same kind of hobbies, or to understand each other perfectly all the time. Hence, some teams shy away from taking anyone different from their own background or nationality. They will still find it hard to get on with the people they have accepted because they have assumed that they will be thinking alike.

When new people come to your team, though they know you are the team leader, often respect is earned and not given. They don't know you, they may not trust you fully yet. Some team leaders may feel that they need to be liked by their new teammates in order for them to listen. At times this can lead to hesitation in giving them the best guidance at the crucial time of their first term on the field. This is especially so if they feel that the new teammates will not like what they hear. Truth is (and this applies to any locals you meet), nobody cares how much you know, until they know how much you care.

Stop seeing your teammates for what they can offer the team, or how you can get onto their 'good side', or hide your past and present mistakes. These are ways for others to lose their trust in you. Instead, aim to find out what it is that God wants for your teammates and pray and work towards it. If they can see how you care about them, they may not yet see the point of your advice, but they will take it on board.

Good things take time. We are quick to rush a process at times because we want to see progress faster than the time it takes to do it properly. The Chinese have a saying about a farmer who couldn't wait for his rice plants to grow tall so he pulled up the shoots that had sprouted to make them taller. They all died soon after. This is a good parable for mentoring new people on the field. People take time to grow, and for some it takes longer than others! Learning language and culture is only the beginning. If you want people to thrive long-term on the field, let them have time to develop and grow before next steps. Don't short-change a teammate's best for what you need out of them – trust the Holy Spirit to work out the right timing and details in God's timeframe. You can see God cares about things done right, not fast.

If you made a movie about a superhero team, what would it look like? The most important job for a team leader is to facilitate an atmosphere in the team that allows everyone to be heard and feel valued, and together to be obedient to the Spirit's prompting. This means that there should not be a dominant culture or personality in the group (e.g. western, or extraverted, or conservative, or Pentecostal). It is not enough to just 'include' the different people in your team and to only to have them sitting in the same room. If you have different cultures on your team (and people from different parts of the U.S. certainly count as different cultures), it means that at any given time there is someone in the team feeling uncomfortable. This also means that if someone is always feeling comfortable (including yourself), it is time to adjust the culture of the team.

Team means people with different backgrounds and sometimes brokenness. Do you want the local fellowship to accept, love, and walk alongside broken people? Then accept some not-so-perfect people onto your team (someone accepted you, right?). Again, it is not enough to be merely willing to 'accept' them onto the team. There needs to be an understanding that it will take more effort to walk alongside them, helping them grow into what God intends for them to be. If you want your local group to be willing to take that extra step in accepting broken people, then you should be committed to working with people who are also broken.

An "Ethos of Grace" (one of Pioneers' core values) is not to condone clearly wrong behaviour, but to recognise that we are all on a journey. It is a willingness to work with people who are trying to move to where God wants them to be. In a place where no gospel has penetrated, there is often a lot of brokenness. You may find that the best witnesses are those most unlikely heroes who faithfully give glory to the Father, daily relying on God because they have to, and giving testimony of hope to those who are also struggling.

Great leaders lead people not where they want to go, but where they ought to go. Another often used saying is to "trust the Holy Spirit's calling in the individual." Some team leaders misunderstand that their job is to merely manage or facilitate people toward that vision. But God reveals His vision step by step as we gain more understanding and as we become more ready to hear. We all have a tendency to put God, His work, and our capacity into boxes. What if God wants us to dream bigger? As team leaders we want to be praying towards the potential of our team and teammates, even to the point of outcomes beyond our imagination.

Stress can bring out the worst and best of us. When we are stressed, we all tend to retreat back to the corner where we feel most comfortable. We sometimes create a boundary around us where we feel safe. We tell ourselves, "I will wait until I'm less stressed and then I will go outside of this circle, once I'm more ok." We then spend a lot of precious energy and money trying to recreate a 'home feeling' of leisure: making western food, looking for that hard-to-get movie, etc. More often than not, we need to be looking for signs that the search for stress relief doesn't become another stress, or simply an escape from the reality.

Sometimes it is precisely in this time of helplessness that one needs to venture out, to ride on what the Holy Spirit has given you and see what He does. As team leaders, it's crucial to try and help your teammates to gain a perspective on what matters. The things that will sustain you long-term is not that DVD or the precious pasta we can't get in the local shop. What sustains us is going to be witnessing how God is working in your area and in the people you meet. No amount of great pizza is going to replace that. Try to encourage people to have less on their plate, and to focus on things that matter.

Pray and work towards that potential in everyone. I hope to see every new local convert as a potential new local church leader. I also hope to mentor my new teammates as potential new team leaders for new teams. This may not be in their vision yet, but I pray and work towards it as such. Usually it takes years for any individual to be ready, but I would pray and dream of this reality from day one. Be it for locals or my teammates, they need a healthy example of team.

To achieve the best of 'team' you need to understand that it is not entirely up to you – the leader – to know and decide the direction of the team. We as a team can pray together to discern His vision together. When you facilitate the process and atmosphere of listening well, you will see a more complete, beautiful picture that God is painting for your team. This picture is going to be way more inspiring than any one person may present.

Openness to be changed and moulded is more important than any skill set. To those recruits that have the picture-perfect resume, with the exact skill set that the team needs – beware! Sometimes it is those people who have a very fixed idea about what they want to do. This can limit God's work inside of them. Going on the field should change us; if it doesn't, then we are of no use to anyone. We will have ignored the biggest work God wants to do – the work within us.

If someone says, "I feel that God is calling me to do...... in......" or, "I want to be doing...... in......," you should question the real motives behind the desire to use certain skill or vocation. At the very least, try to paint a realistic expectation of what it means to be doing a specific job in a new context. I believe that more often than not, God will say, "I want you to be a light in..., using whatever means/skills." Do your recruits have the openness to God to say, "Whatever it takes, including my skills and identity"? Is there an openness to say "Yes, I will go, even if I will need to wait for years before I can see the fruition of that promise"? Are you also prepared to do whatever it takes and find joy in reaching people with the good news?

God is the best teacher, if we choose to listen – better than any university or seminary. Are we willing to be changed by where He has brought us? Even to the point of seeing our theology change, by listening to Him and what He is teaching us in our new culture? Are we tied to our thinking that we are bringing God, or 'modern science' or 'western ways of church' to this new context? Can we have a heart that says, "Teach me and mould me into whatever it takes for me to reach people where you have asked me to be"?

So there you have it; I hope these words will help you one day. I want to leave you with a thought that a wise man once shared with me: When he was young, he was scared about what lay ahead, and he asked God about the future. Toward the end of his life, he realized that for God not to reveal the future when he asked was such a blessing for him, because he would have flat-out refused to go forward if he had known what was ahead. He said, "But what a journey it was! What a companion I had on this journey! I would not have traded it for anything else in the world." This was said by a man who spent thirteen years in a prison labour camp for his faith.

I wonder whether you would go forward if you know the valleys He will take you through. But if you focus on that, then you won't know the splendour of that view along the way, and the heart of the Companion who walks with you. To be a team leader is a thankless job with not many perks and even less holidays. If you do your job right, you may even be more in the background, where God is the one who is glorified and not you. There will be His death that you carry but also His resurrection and transformation. And what a journey it will be! One that gives you an opportunity to grow into the 'you' you have never imagined you can be, with the ultimate Companion who has always believed you could. That will give you more hope in seeing the same for your teammates you serve.

Blessings,
Willow

WEEK 4
DAY 25

Coffee break with Jenn

Jenn Grace was raised in the Northwestern part of America. She moved to East Asia more than 16 years ago where she has lived and worked ever since. Jen has lead a team and served in other leadership roles for the last 12 years.

Dear New Leader,

I thought I might perhaps share with you one lesson that I've learned about leadership. A recent conversation with my son highlighted for me what I've learned.

"Mom, what is the hardest part about leadership?"

I was slightly taken aback. The question had come from my eighteen year old son and, while he's a very sensitive boy, he usually asks questions that I'm prepared to answer. We were cooking dinner together and admittedly the best conversations happen when we're doing something side by side.

A few years ago my answer would have included a quick, "people make the job that much harder." This time I was less sure of how to answer.

Leadership has been one of the tools God has used to shape my character. It has revealed that at my core I am prideful. Pride manifests itself in so many ways. I can listen to someone and think I know what is best for him or her. When someone is burdened, I too am weighed down wondering how I can help and how I can fix his or her situation. When people critique my leadership I can change myself so that others will be satisfied. Unfortunately, my starting and ending point still centers on me. No matter where I turn, I still bump into myself and, unless my reference point changes, this will continue for the remainder of my leadership journey.

So to answer my son's question: the hardest part about leadership is me. I am a piece of work, desperately needing God's grace and mercy. These days, it's less about striving to be, do, or say the right things to gain the approval of others or succeed in my role. I am coming to understand that the crucible of leadership is found at the cross, dying to myself and being made alive in Christ. Daily. It is making mistakes, facing my pride again and again, and releasing myself to God again. It is not being weighed down by shame and condemnation, but believing that the blood of Jesus was and is enough for all of my shame. It is also about journeying together in community, inviting others to speak into my life. It is trusting a handful of spiritual companions who will help lead me to the light when I can't walk there alone.

A leader who walks in humility is one who understands that without the finished work of Christ she would be nothing. She understands that Christ must be the reference point from where we start. She also deeply knows that community is the place where true humility is tested and lived out.

Grace to you in your own leadership journey,
Jenn

Lunch with Dave

David Yebuah has served for 10 years as a cross-cultural missionary in his home country of Ghana. He has been leading his mission team for the last five years.

Dear Leader,

Greetings from Ghana. We're entering the rainy season and this time sees most farmers preparing their land, tilling the soil, and clearing all the ash from bush fires that had happened in the dry season – whether those fires happened by deliberate action or simply an act of nature. It's amazing how the season ushers in new rain that slowly turns the black, charred, and brown dry places of the terrain into lush green foliage.

My very early memories of leadership are borne out of such examples of fathers working the soil and mothers gathering the returns to feed us, a family of seven. However, having grown up in the city, I was bombarded with a different side to leadership – from a strong, disciplined father and a nation that was still under military rule. These aspects of understanding leadership, especially from a male-dominated culture, I realize today will go a long way to shape fundamentally what I thought leadership should be and look like; I must confess, traits that still remain and that I battle with.

My personality as a very introverted individual and more-or-less a pacifist meant I never considered myself as a potential leader; a leader had to be strong, boisterous, hard, and charismatic. These were no attributes of mine.

However, things changed dramatically when I became born again at sixteen. In high school my mentor was both gentle and firm. He walked with me, ate with me, and explained God's Word to me. As I began to see leadership from Christ's perspective, my very persona began to change. My first brush with leadership was when I was made one of the executives of the Christian group in college by my mentor. Soon after this experience I began to serve as a volunteer at age 19 with Pioneers. This was to become part of the very building blocks of my understanding of Christian leadership.

The men and women at Pioneers Africa exhibited a fresh new sense of leadership that my immediate environment had never taught me. It was almost confusing to me. I must say I actually lost myself in their midst. I was taught with gentle strokes but with firm rods. I was counselled with extensive grace but made to understand truth balanced with mercy and love. After almost eighteen years and presently a team leader, I am still learning and still hoping to be a better leader. I see many great men who have gone before me and thank God for their mentorship… I also see in me brokenness that God is using to His glory.

What does it mean to be a mission team leader? I would say: serving from a position of brokenness and knowing that the Father has given me the highest example to emulate in Christ. It means service, it means sacrifice, and it means steadfastness.

What is one message I have heard about team leadership that I disagree with? One that comes to mind is a relativist post-generational argument on democracy and consensus-building. As much as I believe in sharing and agreement and even to a large extent sacrifice of a leader's opinion in the face of popular interest, I believe fundamentally that leadership is very much a theocracy – a theocracy built on solid theology of God's word. In every relativist argument or opinion there is bound to be an absolute position on God's Word. Only it takes grace and truth to balance both.

What do I wish I had known when I was starting out in my role? Hmm… I will say that God can use even broken people. The world would choose 'perfect' men; God will use broken men. Leadership will further break you and point more to God than to you.

If I could go back and write a letter to my younger self, it would be, "Young David, remember always it's not about you, or anyone else. It's about Him and His glory. Let your brokenness move you from self-pity and self-reliance to a place of God reliance – in every sense of the word."

One important lesson I have learnt is that God uses broken people to His glory. One mistake is to think it was about me and relying on my capabilities and less on His provision. My strength through these challenges has moved me from people-reliance to a deep sense of total reliance on Him – a virtue that is still taking shape.

I began this letter by talking of the farmer, my father, and a military ruler. These images, though they shaped somewhat my very early views of leadership, were all part of God's beautiful tapestry that He was weaving to make me understand Him better. It is amazing how a culture of lack and poverty could actually move you to looking to the hills and knowing as a leader your true help comes from the Lord Himself, the Maker of heaven and earth! This for me is the centre of my leadership experience, and it keeps me going. Because I am frail, broken and incapable …but He is strong; and the very thought of that gives me strength.

Thank you for giving me this privilege to share and pour out my heart.

God bless, *shalom*, and *nyame nshira wo* (God bless you)!
Dave

Week 4

Day 26

Coffee break with Shad

Shad Walsh left his home in America for Peru 15 years ago and has served as a leader for the last nine years: four years as a team leader, and the last five as a field leader.

Dear Leader,

Here are a few things I wish I'd known when I started out as a leader:

Be transparent. You'll almost never lose people's respect by being honest about your own struggles and shortcomings. In fact, everyone I've met finds that to be one of the most attractive things in a leader and are drawn to it.

Extend grace. Allow people to find what works best for them and their family. Just because it works for you and the current team, doesn't mean it's the only way. New team members will automatically feel a certain pressure to conform, so don't add to that where not necessary.

Team is valid ministry. Don't see investing in and discipling your team as a distraction from the ministry to the unreached people group (UPG). God has called you to make disciples, and that calling is just as valid within your team as within the UPG.

Invest in your team members. There will come times when you have to make 'withdrawals' in the form of confrontations from within the relationships you have within your team. Be sure to be making 'deposits' into those relationships in order to have footing to be heard and respected during those difficult times.

Be discipled by someone. As a leader there is a tendency to feel isolated and that makes us vulnerable to Satan's attacks. You will deal with temptations and struggles as a leader that require the voice and protection of mentors and accountability partners. It is a wise leader, not a weak one, who puts these structures in place.

Keep good records. All of us are prone to forget or have selective memories as to what we've agreed to. Keep good records of conversations, meetings, and decisions. These will go a long way towards safeguarding good team relationships and productivity.

Blessings in your journey,
Shad

Week 4: Day 26:

Lunch with Keane

Keane Leon was born in Singapore and migrated to Australia with his family as a teenager. With over 10 years of leadership experience before reaching the field five years ago, Keane has been a mission team leader for the last five years.

Dear New Leader,

One of the most enduring battles and obstacles you will face in the future as you seek to serve God as a leader is pride. Yes, pride. Of course you may not think you are a proud person (others may differ) and pride may not seem to be a prominent feature of your life. But believe me, unfortunately, pride is always there. You are not aware because it often disguises itself and rears its ugly head in very subtle and even noble manifestations. It is a silent killer that prowls around to devour many aspiring and seasoned leaders alike. You will find yourself fluctuating between two extremes: righteousness (self) at one end and humility (false) at the other.

So you will ask... what is pride? As I am no theologian or philosopher, and having a more simplistic mind, to me, it's simply, "Look at how great I am!"

In the future, your authority as a leader will be challenged and people will secretly or openly criticise and bad-mouth you. There will be times when no one appreciates or thanks you for your hard work. Some of your team members will usurp your authority or will not submit to you as a leader (although the Bible says they are supposed to). You naturally will feel (but should you?) hurt, indignant, angry, threatened, wrongfully done by; and often a sense of perceived righteousness will well up in you, asking God, "I have done what is the best for them, how come they didn't see it? I am the leader, why don't they show me some respect? How can they criticise me or disagree with me when I am right?" What comes next will be a series of self-righteous responses:

demanding your rights, defending your position, getting others to be on your side, ignoring or obliterating the criticism/people involved. And sadly, your actions often lead to divisions, conflicts, good ideas and suggestions being ignored or buried, and people isolated or forced to leave the team. These are the consequences of pride.

Swinging to the other side of the pendulum, at times when you are asked to lead or when you need to step up and make some tough choices as a leader, doubts will plague you: "Oh no, I cannot do this; they are much better or can do a better job than me; if I make a mistake, what will they think of me?" Of course, sometimes these may be accurate sober judgments on yourself and the situation. However, you will come to realise that, more often than not, the source is usually from a sense of inferiority, inadequacy, and insecurity. And digging deeper, you will find the ugly head of pride rearing itself to the surface again as the focus is still on self, an overwhelming concern of whether I can succeed, and what people will think of me if I don't succeed or if I do make a mistake. Ultimately it is still, "Look how great I am …until you see the real me!" That's why you will shrink from stepping up to the plate and making the tough choices, and instead seek to say what itching ears want to hear for fear of being rejected! It is again pride.

The antidote to pride is Jesus. He has set an example for us to follow. These are the lessons you will learn as you stumble and fall along your way.

As you look to Jesus who forsook His rights to be God, and the great injustice He endured for us (Philippians 2:1-11), what rights can you truly demand: your right to be right? To be respected? To be listened to? To be appreciated? To be asked? Giving up our rights is not easy. Humility is not in our nature. You need to be very sure of three things to be able to learn humility. Jesus was. Before He washed His disciples' feet and headed to the Cross, He was sure of His authority, His identity and His acceptance (John 13:3.)

Jesus knew His authority came from the Father. The Father had put all things under His power. The people saw His authority and could differentiate it from that of the teachers of the law (Mark 1:22, 27.) The teachers of the law had titles and positions but not authority. Your authority is from above. You will never get that respect or approval from people. Even if you did, it will not last.

Jesus knew He had come from God. He knew His true identity. Often your identity is tied to your job title or position, what you can or have done for Him, or how people perceive you. But as you begin to grasp and truly know your true identity as God's child and heir, it will free you of those insecurities and inadequacies so you can be who He wants you to be and not what others want you to be.

Jesus knew He was returning to God. He belongs and is accepted there. That is His future and His home. You too are returning home to God. You are fully accepted by God. Experiencing God's acceptance will help you to stop seeking for cisterns that leak water.

Finally, just like discipleship, leadership is messy, because we are all messy (although redeemed). We go on this journey of sanctification together, to grow to be like Christ. Therefore you will learn from Jeremiah 3:15 that you will need to stay very close to God, pursue His heart. Only then can you lead with His wisdom and understanding. It is so easy to lead with our wisdom and understanding, to follow certain programs, methods, formulas and, more often than not, insist to do things a certain way because it works. This is not wrong as our wisdom and understanding are mainly based on what we or others we know have experienced and tested to work. However you will realise that you can be so attached to our wisdom and understanding (May I give them names like traditions, security blankets, CPMs?) that you can be closed to what God is doing anew. Yes, it is pride again.

Blessings in your journey,
Keane

WEEK 4

Day 27

Coffee break with Patrick

Korean leader, Patrick Kong, moved from America to East Asia over five years ago, and has been serving as a team leader there for the last few years.

Dear New Leader,

Welcome to the world of team leadership! Below you'll find some tips that I've learned and continue to re-learn.

Leaders come in all shapes and sizes. We may come into leadership positions thinking that leaders must have certain gifting. This plays out especially when we start comparing ourselves to other leaders whom we respect, and this type of comparison is not only unhealthy for us, but also for the team as well. Out of our insecurity, we try to exert self-will to be a certain kind of leader, instead of learning to listen to the leading of the Spirit for our team.

It is of utmost importance to create an environment where we are praying to the Father and being led by the Spirit. Doing this at the beginning of team formation is probably the easiest. For a young team that's forming, focus more on establishing these good foundations, and less on hammering away at particular strategies for outreach. Once you get busy with strategies for outreach, it'll be hard to establish these foundations.

Think the best of your teammates. This is especially important at the beginning stages of team formation. Lots of assumptions will be made because people are just getting to know each other. It's so easy to make judgments and become critical. Take a step back (pause), ask good questions, and choose to love.

Really want your teammates to succeed. This sounds like something that doesn't need to be said, but I think if we picture ourselves not simply as their leaders, but also their cheerleaders, we will pray for them, encourage them, and do whatever we can do (within our power and means) so that they can do what our Father has called them to do.

Don't be afraid of conflicts. As a young leader, I remember always trying to smooth things over between teammates so that conflicts wouldn't arise. What a mistake that was! If conflicts exist, don't try to control and manage (or avoid). Trusting that the Father is in the conflict, discern together with others what the Father might be doing and saying. Disagreements and hurts are bound to happen, and the Father will use them to being the team into closer union.

Lead by example. If you want your teammates to love God, you must love God. If you want your teammates to be vulnerable, you must be vulnerable. If you want your teammates to get out there to take risks, you must get out there.

Have fun together. Create shared memories.

Don't be afraid to use your strengths. At the same time, don't be afraid to admit your weaknesses. I've always told people on my team, "I am a big-picture strategist. I love talking and strategizing. But I'm terrible at the actual implementation. I need help putting plans to action."

Help the team keep its eyes upon Jesus. It's so easy for us to get distracted by the day-to-day tasks and responsibilities. Help the team pause, pray together, read the Word together, sing together, or whatever other way that will encourage you all to lift your eyes up to Him.

I hope some of these tips were helpful to you. Of course, the most important thing is to seek the Lord in all things, and invite others in the team to seek Him with you. He is the ultimate team leader, not us! The process of a team growing together and working together is a dynamic process that always changes. It's a journey together that I hope you all find great joy in and richness in relationship.

Blessings
PK

Lunch with Kaylee

Kaylee Dunbar and her husband moved from their home in America to Southeast Asia 17 years ago, where they assumed leadership of their team two years later.

Dear New Leader,

I'm so glad to hear you are learning about leadership, gaining some practical tools. I appreciate that you want some personal insight, too, asking me about my biggest struggle in leadership … well, hands down, it's this:

Leadership has brought me face to face with the real me.

It holds up mirrors. I suppose they are warped and wavy carnival mirrors, made from varying mixtures of truth, perception, and enemy-approved lies. But they showcase shortcomings, and like even the worst mirror, tell me at least something about myself.

Take, for instance, the mirror where I see myself backed against a sky-high measuring stick with markers such as: "Prays her heart out for the people group," "Serves her team wholeheartedly," and "Loves the people like Jesus would." I'm not even close.

Another mirror reflects a crowd of disappointed-looking people around me, thought bubbles floating above their heads: "Why don't you go out weekly with us?" "Why don't you ever have us over for lunch?" and, "Why don't you check in on me?" How can I live up?!

And step right up to a third mirror: an array of clay pots – beautiful ones, big ones, distinct ones. Yet the one directly in front of me, my own reflection, is this tiny little thing. Frustratingly fragile and seemingly low-capacity. I can't even meet my own standards.

I am surrounded by all that I am not. I'm in a house of mirrors, and everywhere I see the reflection of my flaws.

But praise the Lord. Because bit by bit, after 15 years of paranoid mirror-watching, He's shining His truth on the distortions of the mirrors – and using them as powerful instruments in my life. He's uncovering the lies they represent. He's revealing the sins of self-effort that nullifies grace, of pride that wants me to look good, of fear of man instead of fear of God, of just plain unbelief.

And He's opened my mind to the truth that I've often ignored the work in my life of the One who called me into leadership. I've believed what looks believable instead of Who is believable: Jesus, the reflection of the glory of God; the Author and Perfector of our faith. The true mirror.

But some things could've helped me earlier on.

First, having a mentor from the get-go – someone who knew me, or someone who would stick with me despite, well… me. With her in place, I would determine to be teachable, come what may … knowing God has put her in that position to teach me Christlikeness.

I'd be willing to take an honest look at all of me in the light of God's truth, and let Him determine what goes in the Save and Discard boxes. Maybe something I've concealed the Lord wants to redeem. Maybe something I've liked about myself is 'all about me' and needs to be destroyed.

I would ask people about my strengths, so I could maximize them. And my flaws and sinful tendencies, so I could face them. Bring it on: name them, so I can deal with them.

I would go through – put in writing – my stories of shame and regret and fear and anger and pull out all the threads of truth that God has revealed; because it's with these that He'll make a beautiful tapestry to glorify His Name. These are the treasures of darkness.

I am learning to fight those same areas: shame, regret, fear, anger, etc., with the sword of truth, memorizing, reviewing, and writing it on the doorposts of my house …so that I can live victoriously.

I would familiarize myself with a system for meaty study of God's Word. This is how I will know Him and His ways.

From the beginning, I would consistently be reading a book about God's character or the Gospel. I want who He is and what He has done, is doing, to be my greatest joy.

I would find a way – accountability, setting patterns, developing habits – to make sure I was choosing to believe ...so that I would push through anything with rock-solid faith that "God in His goodness willed it."

I would remember that the things I struggle with in others are possibly the very things they struggle within themselves. Every person is facing a battle. "God gives us discernment to make us prayerful, not critical." If so-and-so's arrogance is driving me nuts... pray for his (and my) humility.

I would be encouraged: to know that, whether a 'natural' leader or not, it is possible to grow as one, and a worthy pursuit indeed. But let God do His work in my deepest character ...above all else. And then... watch Him do it in others. All of us together, from glory to glory. Praise Him for it.

I haven't escaped the mirrors. But God is gently turning my eyes away from the lie-encrusted reflections – all those keenly-felt insecurities and shortcomings – to the pure and true image of all that God is for us in Christ Jesus: life, godliness, grace, forgiveness, power... and whatever else leadership will require. When we fix our eyes on Him, He'll transform us into His perfect image. Him, or the carnival mirror? No question.

"For now we see only a reflection as in a mirror; then we shall see face to face" (1 Corinthians 13:12.)

With great hope,
Kaylee

Day 28

Day of Reflection...

Take a moment to reflect on the 'conversations' of the last 6 days...

- *What portions of the letters did you underline? What struck you or jumped out at you?*
- *Is there anything you disagreed with or would like to have further discussion about?*
- *What themes seem to be standing out to you? How do these things tie together?*
- *Sit for a few minutes and ask the Lord, What would you have me walk away with and take to heart or implement? With whom would you have me discuss this?*

Week Five

WEEK 5

Day 29

Coffee break with Yousef

Yousef Nassar has nearly 3 decades of ministry experience include 19 years in leadership both in his native Egypt and his adopted country, the United Kingdom.

Dear Ministry Colleague,

Before I start sharing my thoughts with you, I would like to confess that I wasn't the best leader in my ministry. This may be because of my family and work background before I had been called by the Lord to work in ministry, or perhaps because of the lack of spiritual formation in my early Christian life. Sometimes I look back, think about the different stages of my life, and feel sad for not doing better to enjoy the wonderful life with my Lord in a better way. At the same time, as a new Christian, we only learn what we are taught.

It took me a long time to start writing these words. I was struggling between several ideas to share about. I wanted to put everything I went through in it, but when I start typing this letter, I was focusing on one issue.

I started working with our mission organization just after we arrived to the UK coming from Egypt, becoming a full member about 16 years ago. The team was new, actually was the first ministry team in the UK. We were very excited to start the work in this cosmopolitan large city, with the ability to speak at least three or four different languages in doing the work and most of us had a huge experience in reaching the target people. It was awesome. For the first two years, I was trying to learn more about the British culture, improving my English, and going everywhere to do ministry. However, I did not feel the connection between the team leader and myself. He understood the Moroccan culture very well. He can speak the Moroccan accent too. He has enough experience. Nevertheless, I am an Egyptian, not a Moroccan man.

We never tuned together. He dealt with me as if he was dealing with a Moroccan person. I was not a Moroccan. I am an Egyptian. I think differently than a Moroccan; I live differently too. For many years, we were in the same situation. Until I asked some friend who have long experience in both Morocco and in Egypt for help. He was able to understand where the problem was coming from and was able to advise my team leader, telling him that Yousef is not a Moroccan and he came from a different culture.

I believe that the main disagreement came from the poor leadership. My team leader did not take any initiative to come closer and ask me how we think as an Egyptian in different situations. Yes, we are all Arabs and came from the same geographic area in the world, but we are completely different people.

Understanding my team members is one of the most important matters to lead in harmony. We can successfully waste time, effort and lose great team members by ignoring how much we are different. I believe there are many team leaders who have enough pride to do the same mistake many times. My prayer is that everyone will learn from other people's mistakes.

Grace,
Yousef

WEEK 5 : DAY 29 :

Lunch with Paul

Paul Rednib followed God's call to Mongolia from America 21 years ago. He has served in leadership there for the last 15 years including team and now field leadership.

Dear Leader,

Working together with people can be very challenging. I have heard friends from various walks of life say, "I love my work; it's the people that I work with who drive me crazy." Quite honestly, I have occasionally felt that way myself. People who grew up in the same culture, community, even the same family, find working together difficult; how much more those who come from completely different cultural backgrounds? One would think in our line of work that this wouldn't be an issue. After all, we all have a specific goal in mind that we have been called by God to work together to meet.

As Pioneers teams, we seek to glorify God among unreached peoples by initiating church planting movements in partnership with local churches. This is a pretty specific goal. We should all be able to be on the same page on this one. So why is there so much struggle to get along? Why is it that we see new people come to the field with passion and excitement to be a part of this great calling only to see them become hurt, and have those good emotions turn to cynicism and bitterness toward fellow teammates? How easy it is to get off course. Far too often at the practical level we lose sight of the goal and let lesser, somewhat insignificant, issues rob us of our vision. How can we encourage people to stay on course? How can we stand strong even when our expectations are crushed? How can we see multicultural teams beautifully displaying the glory of Christ as they work together in unity? I believe that God has the answers to these questions, and that we can find them as we look in His Word. In this letter, I want to simply explore a few Scriptural principles which I hope will help in maintaining the right perspective with our eyes on the goal.

In 1 Peter 2:9-10 we are told, "But you are a chosen race, A royal priesthood, a holy nation, a people for God's own possession, so that you may proclaim the excellencies of Him who has called you out of darkness into His marvelous light; for you once were not a people, but now you are the people of God; you had not received mercy, but now you have received mercy." Notice that it doesn't say that you are a chosen being, a royal priest, a holy individual, a person for His own possession. He has made us His people, His community so that we may proclaim His excellencies. We best make Him known, we best bring glory to Him, as we function together in community. As those who are God's people, we are not to view each other with eyes of judgment. Treating each other with mercy is a key part of this community because we all have received the life-changing mercy of God. We must guard our hearts against having an attitude of criticism toward one another. It is really easy to fall into that trap. The glue that holds this community together is love. Love always seeks for the good for each other, which leaves no room for hurtful attitudes. "Love is patient, love is kind. It does not envy, it does not boast, it is not proud. It does not dishonor others, it is not self-seeking, it is not easily angered, it keeps no record of wrongs. Love does not delight in evil but rejoices with the truth. It always protects, always trusts, always hopes, always perseveres. Love never fails" (1 Corinthians 13:4-8a.) God is love, and as His chosen race, this love should define us. For the world to see His glory, they must see this love lived out in our community.

In John 17:20-23 Jesus prays to the Father concerning this community. "My prayer is not for them alone. I pray also for those who will believe in me through their message, that all of them may be one, Father, just as you are in me and I am in you. May they also be in us so that the world may believe that you have sent me. I have given them the glory that you gave me, that they may be one as we are one – I in them and you in me – so that they may be brought to complete unity. Then the world will know that you sent me and have loved them even as you have loved me." The message we so eagerly desire for the world around us to know is only really effectually communicated as we work together in the unity that only His glory can bring. Being team isn't just a nice idea, it is in the heart of God that we become perfectly one. What are we telling the world about our God if we cannot get along? How will we see His glory revealed to the nations if we walk outside of His intended purpose? We are not His bodies, we are His Body, and as such we are one, and must work together in that oneness. Anything else is really misrepresenting Him.

It seems that as people chosen by God and deeply in love with Jesus that walking together with each other in unity would not be a problem. In fact, it should be a fairly natural outcome. Yet the Scripture tells us to work at it. "As a prisoner for the Lord, then, I urge you to live a life worthy of the calling you have received. Be completely humble and gentle; be patient, bearing with one another in love. Make every effort to keep the unity of the Spirit through the bond of peace. There is one body and one Spirit, just as you were called to one hope when you were called; one Lord, one faith, one baptism; one God and Father of all, who is over all and through all and in all" (Ephesians 4:1-6.) With all the 'oneness', why do we need to be implored to be diligent to preserve the unity? Maybe, just maybe, we far too often forget about humility. I know that I do. It is not that I forget the concept of humility, it is just that pride surfaces in so many subtle, and sometimes blatant, ways. The thing is that focusing on me will never bring humility. Only by focusing on Jesus and on others do I actually lose myself.

We have the perfect example of this: "Therefore if there is any encouragement in Christ, if there is any consolation of love, if there is any fellowship of the Spirit, if any affection and compassion, make my joy complete by being of the same mind, maintaining the same love, united in spirit, intent on one purpose. Do nothing from selfishness or empty conceit, but with humility of mind regard one another as more important than yourselves; do not merely look out for your own personal interests, but also for the interests of others. Have this attitude in yourselves which was also in Christ Jesus, who, although He existed in the form of God, did not regard equality with God a thing to be grasped, but emptied Himself, taking the form of a bond-servant, and being made in the likeness of men. Being found in appearance as a man, He humbled Himself by becoming obedient to the point of death, even death on a cross" (Philippians 2:1-8.) Where would we be without this example? Do I have His attitude? Am I intent on the right purpose? Am I pure in heart, single-focused, or is double-mindedness a problem? Selfishness and conceit destroy fellowship and community. A good barometer for me is this question: "Am I more concerned for what I want, or for the true needs of others?" I have mastered the selfish thing. For me, that was pretty easy. But I have to work, and work hard at having the attitude of Christ.

God created us for relationship with Him – for vibrant, life-giving, joy-filled, peaceful, loving relationship where we continually interact with Him concerning everything that is on our heart. He created community for us, with Himself, with family, and with the church, His Body. I think too often we forget that we have a very real enemy. Satan seeks to bring destruction to the good that God has created. Jesus tells us that, "The thief comes only to steal and kill and destroy; I have come that they may have life, and have it to the full" (John 10:10.) Our enemy is not nice. "He was a murderer from the beginning, not holding to the truth, for there is no truth in him. When he lies, he speaks his native language, for he is a liar and the father of lies" (John 8:44b.) 1 Peter 5:8 tells us that our enemy prowls around like a roaring lion, seeking someone to devour. Since community is so important to God, what do you think is Satan's strategy? He only desires to kill, steal, and destroy. He uses any and every device he can imagine to rob us from living in community. He sets traps and deludes us to think his way is better. He uses greed, selfishness, pride, immorality, lust, bitterness, longings for significance, desires for things that others have …anything to rob us from the good relationships that God desires for us. Just look at what happened in the garden. Adam and Eve used to walk with God, in incredible communion with Him. After they listened to Satan they hid from Him. Were they happier, more fulfilled, in a better place for listening to him? No – it only brought brokenness and destruction. Instead of being there for each other, their first response was to blame each other. Sin brought separation from God, and separation from God leaves us broken and empty.

Satan's strategy is to destroy the community that God has created for good. We see that happening all around in families and in churches. We must be aware of what he is doing. Could it be that my struggle with a teammate is more than just a personality issue? Could it be that my attitude toward my wife is deeper than, "If she would only…"? If Satan can break up our families and disrupt our community, he then renders us ineffective at proclaiming the glory of God. We need to be proactive on this, not reactive. Our enemy is good at what he does. Our Savior is infinitely better.

Ephesians 6 tells us that our struggle is not with each other, but against spiritual forces of evil. Far too often we find ourselves fighting against each other. When we do that we fall right into his trap designed to make us ineffectual. We cannot avoid that trap in our own strength. We are told to stand strong in the Lord and in the strength of His might. We are told to put on His armor. Then we are told to pray. To see the light of the glorious Gospel of Jesus penetrate the darkness, prayer is essential. Jesus always did the will of the Father, and He spent hours talking with Him. A praying community is a strong community. It is hard to be truly unified if we don't pray together. I think the single most important thing we can pass on is the God-honoring aroma of prayer permeating our community. It is as incense ascending to the Father, which He out of love and mercy responds to.

We are all broken and needy people. A community of broken and needy people can have a lot of problems. We are also a special people to whom mercy has been given. His mercy overcomes the problems and makes us whole. It is a walk of faith, believing that His way is the right way. The evil one wants us to believe his lies. He wants us to be isolated and self-focused. He wants us to live in never-ending conflict with each other. There is a war being waged to keep us from true community living. Satan is desperate to keep the glory of God from being seen through the unity of His Body. As we fight the good fight, let us remember who we are, what we are called to, and where our strength comes from. Let us be diligent to preserve the unity of the Spirit so that the world will know that Jesus was sent by the Father. May the glory of Jesus be clearly seen through the community of our teams, and may the world be drawn by the power of His love as they see it at work in and through us.

Blessings,
Paul

WEEK 5

Day 30

Coffee break with Jack

Jack MacDonald left his home in America and followed God's call to China where he served for seven years, five of those as a team leader.

Dear Friend,

There are so many ideas about leadership out there right now. It can be difficult to sort through what will be most helpful and then to actually take the time to absorb and ultimately adopt these ideas as part of your own leadership style. I just wanted to pass on a few things that are biblically-based ideas that certainly have far-reaching implications for a broader audience, but are especially important for leaders.

We really only have so much time to focus on the most important things. But if we do not figure out what those things are, there is always something else pulling us in other urgent directions. When it comes to Christ's Kingdom, the most important thing about leadership is knowing that we are not leading anyone anywhere … sexcept leading them to Christ, to follow Him and His directions for their lives and ministry. Our job is to serve Christ and serve them. In order to do this, we ourselves need to be 'set aside' for His work, devoted and consecrated. That is the essence of holiness. We ourselves need to be holy just as He is holy (Leviticus 11, 19, 20; 1 Peter 1:16.)

To be holy devoted (or wholly devoted), it is crucial that we stay plugged into the vine (John 15.) Remaining connected to Jesus as our life source is the essence of devotion. Without staying connected to Jesus, we will not be full of His life. We will not be able to help lead anyone to Jesus. There's nothing that we will do that will be of lasting value without remaining in Him. That is the core of being holy through devotion.

We not only need to be devoted, we also need to be consecrated. There are two parts to being consecrated as holy. The first part is being set apart from sin. This is often what many people think of when they think of holiness. We ought to be religious about this (James 1:27.) However, another part of being holy means to be set apart to God, for His uses and purposes (Romans 12:1, 2.) In John 17:19 Jesus says, "For them I sanctify myself, that they too may be truly sanctified." The term "sanctify" is from a Greek word meaning to be separate from profane things and dedicated to God. So, we need to keep ourselves from sin and we need to consecrate ourselves to Him so that we can be useful to His purposes.

I wish I had known the value of brotherhood/sisterhood and honest gut-checks with friends who can call you out and who you can call out as well. Make sure that you have these. You cannot stay holy without community (1 Peter 2:9.) Community is crucial to staying set apart for God's service. The enemy's attacks are strong. You will be tempted. Make sure that you are constantly open with someone about everything. Sometimes you might feel like you do not have anyone on your team to do that with. Sometimes it is good to find someone outside your team. I remember a married guy whose team was all women for a time. He needed to find someone outside of his team to connect with in order to stay set apart.

You will make mistakes, but keep in mind the key issue of holiness. If you continually seek God, He will make your paths straight. He will show you what His good, pleasing, and perfect will is.

I'm hoping that keeping these things in mind will help you in the long run. Mission work is not a sprint; it takes time. Staying holy and connected to Jesus is so vital. I hope that you will find joy in connecting to others and that keeping accountable will be a joy. Without these, the work will be hindered and nothing eternal will be accomplished.

Blessings!
Jack

Lunch with Dan

Daniel Ross, originally from Australia, has been leading a mission team in East Asia for the last seven years and has recently become a field leader as well.

Dear New Team Leader,

I have two main ideas I want to share with you about leadership, and as I think about it, they were things that were shared with me when I first became a team leader; God has used them to not only shape me as a leader but also as a person. It is obvious that there is so much more that could be said about godly leadership, but this is what I believe God has put on my heart to share at this time.

Firstly, I want to set before you a very high goal; and secondly, a wonderfully comforting truth. The very high goal in leadership is to imitate our Lord Jesus Christ and to call others to imitate you as you imitate Him. I don't just mean look at how Jesus led and copy His example of servant leadership, though that is true. I mean seek to be Christ-like in every area of your life. Be the kind of person you desire the people you lead to be. I know that might almost sound narcissistic, and yes I know people have different personalities and backgrounds and we are not all the same; but even with that in mind, I urge you as a leader, live a life worthy of imitation.

A large part of your leadership is by example. The writer of the book of Hebrews writes to the recipients of his letter, "Remember your leaders, who spoke the word of God to you. Consider the outcome of their way of life and imitate their faith" (Hebrews 13:7.) Paul urges Timothy, "Don't let anyone look down on you because you are young, but set an example for the believers in speech, in conduct, in love, in faith and in purity" (1 Timothy 4:12.) These verses show that in Scripture those who follow are urged to follow the example of their leaders and those who lead are to set an example. Paul famously urges the Corinthian believers to, "Follow my example, as I follow the example of Christ" (1 Corinthians 11:1.) He says this in the conclusion of his discussion on eating meat sacrificed to idols, after stating that his principle is to do all for the glory of God and to not seek his own advantage, so that others might be saved. He has shown them how he behaves in a situation, explained why, and then calls them to do the same. He is leading them.

I remember at one time my feeling about Paul saying "follow my example, as I follow the example of Christ" was that at worst, Paul was perhaps overly arrogant, or at best he did lead such a Christ-like life that it was appropriate for him to make that claim; but that for the rest of us it would be supremely arrogant to do so. Over the years my thinking has changed. Jesus' words to His disciples after modelling servanthood to them were, "I have set you an example that you should do as I have done for you" (John 13:15.) Jesus wants them to follow His example – and His example was to lead by example.

If you are in any kind of Christian leadership and when you look at your life your summary thought is, "I wouldn't want anyone else to be this way," then you need to ask yourself if you are fit to lead. As leaders we need to examine ourselves, and where we see things not worthy of imitation we need to believe the truth of the gospel that in Christ our sins are forgiven; and then we are to repent, that is, turn from our non-Christ-like behaviour and live in a way that more closely matches Christ.

Here I am not only talking about the obvious outward things that others will easily observe, but I am also talking about the inner secret areas of our hearts. It is possible to have all the practical skills of leadership, to know the Bible back to front, to be able to teach God's Word wonderfully, to lead others to Christ, but to actually be living in a way that denies the truth of the gospel. Paul writes to Titus about people who "claim to know God, but by their actions they deny him. They are detestable, disobedient and unfit for doing anything good" (Titus 1:16.) If we profess that Christ, through His death and resurrection, has set us free from the power of sin, yet we live our lives nurturing secret hidden sins, feeding them, enslaved to them ...is our life not a denial of the gospel?

Live in such a way that, along with Paul, you can say to those you lead, "Follow my example, as I follow the example of Christ." I want to finish this point with two verses written by Paul to younger leaders:

"Those who cleanse themselves from the latter will be instruments for special purposes, made holy, useful to the Master and prepared to do any good work" (2 Timothy 2:21.)

"In everything set them an example by doing what is good. In your teaching show integrity, seriousness and soundness of speech that cannot be condemned, so that those who oppose you may be ashamed because they have nothing bad to say about us" (Titus 2:7-8.)

The second point I want to make is a wonderfully comforting truth. That is, the task of being a truly Christ-like leader is beyond you, but it is not beyond God to use you. It is good to recognise our inability at the outset. Paul writes, "For we are to God the pleasing aroma of Christ among those who are being saved and those who are perishing. To the one we are an aroma that brings death; to the other, an aroma that brings life. And who is equal to such a task?" (2 Corinthians 2:15-16) He is talking about being the fragrance of Christ to all around him, believers and non-believers alike, representing Jesus to others. That is what Christian leaders are called to do. Paul's comment is "who is sufficient" to do that? It is a rhetorical question. The answer is meant to be, "no one is sufficient for that!" Don't be tempted to think that you are up to the task of being the fragrance of Christ to others. You aren't.

David writes in Psalm 103:13-14, "As a father has compassion on his children, so the Lord has compassion on those who fear him; for he knows how we are formed, he remembers that we are dust." You are weak, sinful and limited in wisdom; and yet God in His wisdom, so His glory can be seen, can use you to lead others. God knows you better than you know yourself, He remembers that you are dust and has compassion on you. You will fall short and you will fail God, others, and yourself. When you do, preach the gospel to yourself.

God knows that your time and energy are limited. Another wise leader reminded me that God gives us exactly the time needed in a day to do the good works he desires for us to do in that day. If we are always feeling there is not enough time to accomplish what we want to accomplish in a day, then perhaps what we want to accomplish in a day is not in line with what God wants us to accomplish. God remembers that we are dust.

Remembering our weakness will lead us to increased humility in our leadership, it will elevate our desire to pray for ourselves and others, and drive us to have faith in the loving God who is in control.

I love the account of Jesus feeding the five thousand in Luke, chapter 9. Jesus has taken the disciples to a wilderness area for a spiritual retreat after a short-term mission trip, but a crowd has found them. The weary disciples ask Jesus to send the hungry people to the closest village so they can get something to eat. Jesus response is, "You give them something to eat." Why say that? I think He wants them to realise they can't do it. There are over five thousand people and they have a bit of bread and a couple of fish. But then Jesus takes what they have, blesses it, and then verse 16 tells us He gave the bread and fish to the disciples to set before the crowd. Then you know the rest: they all ate and there were leftovers. If I were to ask you, "Who fed the five thousand?" your first response is probably "Jesus", and that isn't wrong. But do you also see that it was the disciples who literally gave the crowd their food? Jesus wanted them to see the task was impossible for them, but then He went and used them for that task. May it be the same for you and me!

With love, your brother in Christ
Daniel

Week 5

Day 31

Coffee break with Olau

Olau Thomassen moved from his native land of Denmark to the United Kingdom as a young man. Three years ago Olau answered God's call to missions and leadership simultaneously and currently serves as both a team and field leader in the United Kingdom.

Hello Dear Sister,

I'm excited that you have decided to accept the team leader role – you've got a lot of fun and challenges ahead!

How do you feel about the appointment? Are you confident or scared out of your wits? A bit of both perhaps? My first encouragement to you is not to delve too much into the reasons you were chosen for the role. Asking that question usually only leads you down one of two unhelpful roads. You may look at your character and gifts, and pridefully conclude that you are perfectly gifted for the role. This view usually leads to lack of fervent prayer, and a hard landing when things do not go your way despite your gifts. Alternatively, you look at your character and gifts, and conclude that you are hopelessly under-qualified, and you may shy back from fully throwing yourself into the role God has given you. I encourage you to simply rest in the fact that God has called you. God consistently delights in using the weak and the vulnerable. Irrespective of your gifts, He can and will work through you, and it gets a lot easier if you are able to take your eyes off yourself and instead focus on Him.

That brings me to my second encouragement. Consistently seek to find your identity in Christ, rather than in your performance or the performance of your team. When I stepped into the area leader role, I quickly grew stressed because I noticed that not every team in my area seemed to be in line with the mission statement of Pioneers. I thought of different ways I could help teams get 'into line', because I wanted to be able to point to my area and say, "Look how amazing my area is – everyone is fully on track with the Pioneers mission." But seeking to find identity in the outward appearance of the area kept me from truly loving the team leaders and team coordinators I was meant to serve. I was not able to simply come alongside them and ask, "How might I love and serve you today?" Instead, I had my own agenda. I needed them to do certain things, so that I could feel good about myself. They became a means to an end. But my regional leader gave me a wise word: "A servant does not have an agenda …he simply asks 'how may I serve?'" and I have gradually begun to enjoy the freedom that comes from simply loving people. I may still have hard conversations from time to time, but they are motivated more by love than they were three years ago. However, living in the freedom to love people only comes when we know we are truly loved by the Father. You are fully free to love your team members when you know that the Father takes great delight in you, even if your team appears to be failing, even if no one is coming to Christ and your team members are struggling with persistent patterns of sin.

Which brings me to my last encouragement. Ask the Father daily to protect your relationship with Him. Ask Him to draw you back when busyness threatens to rob you of your precious time sitting with Him and His Word. Ask Him to draw you back when you have gone off seeking your comfort and hope in the false promises of idols. This will happen, but the Father is so gracious and loving; He will draw you back. Everything I have written earlier in my letter relies on you journeying closely with the Father. Only when you are consistently reminded of the Father's outrageous love for you, and sense the sweet smell of His presence by His Spirit, will you be enabled to live a life free from an unhealthy focus on yourself and desperate attempts to gain approval through the performance of your team. You are free to love ...and that my dear sister, is the good life!

I will be praying for you.
Olau

Lunch with Mike

Mike Welch has nearly 20 years of leadership experience, including the season when he moved from California to China where he and his family lived for 13 years, nine of those as a mission team leader.

Dear Future Leader,

Leadership is a skill you do not currently possess. But, there is hope! God knows you don't know how to do this. He knows how thoroughly inadequate you feel. And yet He has called you to this role. He knows what He is about in asking you to do something that you have not done before. You will fail at times. But you will also succeed at times.

Commit yourself to learning the skill of leadership and at the same time learn to let Him guide you through what is essentially a spiritual endeavor. That means reading books (start with Lead Right by Steve Ventura and Effective Pastoring by William Lawrence). It means talking to those who have become good leaders and who understand what it will mean for a novice like you to walk that road (again, start with Bill Lawrence). It means asking God for direction, wisdom, strength, creativity, courage, and stamina. It means letting Him supply you with what you need and then believing Him that He has given you what you need. Though it probably won't feel like He's given you nearly enough, He has; trust Him. He's done this before, you haven't. Not many will know how to help you. When you expect that someone should be able to help you but they can't/don't/won't, be gracious; they are on the road, too. If the Lord knows you really need another human to come alongside you He'll raise one up. If He does not raise up another then He is asking you to rely solely, directly on Him.

If you are to become a good leader, which you can become – you are God's choice! – It will mean you must grow into someone different than you are now. Change is hard work. And it is uncommon. As

Lawrence points out, your skill as a leader cannot grow beyond your character. It is one thing to look like you are growing; it is another thing entirely to actually change. To actually change will require you to grow in skill and in character.

Recognize that there are many good solutions to most problems or challenges you will face. In the end, you must decide. That's what leaders do. Not everyone will like your decisions and that is okay. But God has put you in the position of leader and He will work through your decisions to bring about His will in your team. Yes, give your team a say. Really listen to what they are saying. Often times, the people you lead want to know you have heard them – heard their hearts, not just their ideas – even more than they want you to adopt their ideas. If they know they've been heard but you make a decision they don't like, they are more likely to be okay with it than if they don't feel like you heard them. I hope that you all have someone like my friend Paul; he is the best leader you will see on the field at doing this. Find someone like Paul and learn from him.

You must have a vision for your team. Why does your team exist? You must communicate this vision, often and in various ways. What is your organization's mission statement and core values? Repeat these often, too. Evaluate your performance against these values. Be honest about where the gaps are and then start working on those. You will feel like you are being condescending by repeating these messages. Do it anyway. The people you lead want to know where they are headed. They need to hear that you are committed to this direction, too. My friend Eric is the best leader you will see on the field at doing this. Find someone like Eric and learn from him.

Do not criticize one team member to another. Do not criticize one leader to another leader, and certainly not to a team member. Ever. Nothing will destroy trust faster.

To those who are married and/or have children, love your spouse and your kids. Your commitment to them, your ministry to them, will often be in concert with ministry to those you're working with outside the home, but it is really a prior commitment. Make sure you minister to them, too. There will be many days when you feel worn down and those smiling, accepting, glad-to-see-you faces will minister deeply to you.

Communicate expectations to your team and then hold them accountable for meeting those expectations. Make the expectations achievable by humans (share the gospel with five people, learn 100 new words, recite 10 verses in the target language, or whatever). The goals you have for each team member when added together and accomplished should result in meeting your overall goals for the team. The ultimate hope is that God will take your efforts and accomplish His saving work, but when and how He does that is His alone to decide.

Be selective about who joins the team. Life on the field generally consumes most of the margin in our lives that is normally reserved to buffer us from daily stresses. If people already have depleted margins they usually struggle to just live on the field, and as a result have little to offer to lost and hurting people. You will see this played out most often in people with a history of depression, mood disorders, etc. These issues are too complex to be addressed in the places you will live. You will see one person overcome this without going home. You will see many more that need to go home to get these issues tended to. Be careful with sexual sin, defiance, and divisiveness. In situations that go bad, you will usually find one of these running unchecked.

Send home the ones who cease to be effective.

Don't let people go to a new city without team members in the pipeline who have committed to joining them.

In everything you do, whether it's family, team, or yet-to-believe friends, make loving well your aim.

Grace to you,
Mike

WEEK 5
Day 32

Coffee break with Steve

Steve Currey's mission career spans nearly three decades and has taken him from his home in America to Africa and Europe. During this time he has had numerous leadership responsibilities including team, field, and organizational roles.

Dear Emerging Leader,

You've stepped forward to accomplish an impossible task: lead a group of individualistic, postmodern, diverse, headstrong adults. You've got no salaries to hang over their heads. You've never been this way before and your 'expertise' is most likely just above theirs.

Many of your teammates will have had bad experiences with former leaders, which they will project on to you. You won't live up to their expectations. You'll be expected to meet their unrealistic demands. And when things don't work out, it will be your fault. You'll suggest things which will be refused until a time later when those things you've suggested suddenly become of their own invention. You'll not sleep, sometimes for weeks. Oh… did I mention the daunting task of convincing an entire people group to leave their current religious practices, some of which are thousands of years old, and follow your God?

You'll cry, you'll weep, you'll question yourself, and you'll get angry, perhaps furious… Those things you wrestled with, those besetting sins, will come back to haunt you in your darkest hours.

Hopefully, rather soon, you'll really get to the end of your resources – I know you can assent to that in theory, but, what I'm talking about is living it.

When your spiritual, emotional, and physical resources are done, hopefully you'll look up and hopefully you'll see the risen Christ.

Once you've lived true depravity you'll realize you need something outside of yourself to save you, something totally other. By then you'll know that you've not one ounce of righteousness to offer anyone, certainly not God. By faith you'll ask Him for His righteousness.

And, this… this is right where the Master wants you as a leader. When your resources are gone, by faith you'll need His. You'll long for Him. You'll thirst for Him. And, when you do, He will be found by you. You'll eagerly desire to rise before the dawn and spend time with Him. He will be the only thing that makes sense sometimes. You might not have the language skills to do the things you did as a 5-year old, so your sense of achievement will come from knowing Him. Journal. Meditate. Worship. This is what John 15 abiding in Jesus looks like. And, this is where a leader bears fruit, and the fruit you'll bear from this place of desperation and communion with Him is an enduring fruit.

Hopefully, He'll not let you get 'good' at leadership… Otherwise, you'll have to start all over again.

Your fellow leader,
Steve

Lunch with Adam

Adam Itheni, an American, currently serves in North Africa and has spent 12 of his 14 years on the mission field as a team leader.

Dear Mission Team leader,

Twelve years ago, we started our organization's first church-planting team in North Africa. One year later, we finally landed and wandered out of the airport alone, soon to take an unreasonably expensive taxi ride. Our one contact didn't meet us at the airport. We did not speak the languages. But we knew our stinky, cold, dirty hotel with a shared hallway bathroom would not make a good home, so by faith we prayed and left it, seeking His providence.

Language was only the beginning of our weakness. We'd taken a brief course on Islam, but knew almost nothing about the culture, legal contracts, medical care, how to start a company, how to get visas, what to say to the police, etc. And we sure didn't know how to start churches in an Islamic police state.

But we had peeked at the end of The Book (Revelation 7:9-10), and knew that people from every tongue, tribe, and nation will worship our Lord, so we moved forward with expectancy that the Gospel is the power of God. And to His glory, God has done more than we could have asked or imagined, shattering the nation's ancient assumptions and self-perceptions, and prompting multitudes of disillusioned Arabs to seek truth!

My strongest recommendation to you is that you peek at the end of The Book, too, and base all your confidence on what you find there.

If you'd consider them, though, I would commend to you a few more portions of the Bible.

What Satan said to Adam and Eve (about their potential to be like God in knowing good from evil) was true (Genesis 3:5.) What

Satan said to Jesus (about the stones becoming bread or being able to have the kingdoms at that moment) was true (Matthew 4:4, 4:6, 4:9.) And what Satan will say to you (about being a sinner, about being lustful, about being selfish, about being weak, about not being fully aligned with your values, etc.) will be true, too. But he can and will go to Hell with his truth. What we care about is the truth that God says about us! We are children of God, and what we will be has not yet been made known. But we know that when Christ appears, we shall be like him, for we shall see him as he is (1 John 3:2!) His divine power has given us everything we need for a godly life through our knowledge of him who called us by his own glory and goodness. Through these he has given us his very great and precious promises, so that through them you may participate in the divine nature, having escaped the corruption in the world caused by evil desires (2 Peter 1:3-4!) We are a new creation. The old has passed away and the new has come (2 Corinthians 5:17!) We are a chosen people, a royal priesthood, a holy nation, God's special possession, that you may declare the praises of him who called you out of darkness into his wonderful light (1 Peter 2:9!) There is now no condemnation for those who are in Christ Jesus (Romans 8:1!)

Related: Joseph, Moses, David, Jesus, and Paul, the leaders you most admire, went through absolute misery. It is wonderful when everything you attempt is blessed and multiplying and growing; but do not equate suffering, rebellious followers, hardship, misery, or even death with a lack of God's call on your life (Hebrews 11:32-40.)

Talk to your boss about what dimensions of your job description are truly priorities and non-negotiables. Most organizations' team leader job descriptions have developed in response to decades' worth of problems, and I kind of doubt the Apostle Paul could fulfil them (or that he'd want to). Moreover, in most cases, even if the job description could be faithfully fulfilled, it would be no guarantee that your vision (Matthew 22:37-39) would be accomplished.

Invest in resources (technology, administrative help, etc.) that boost your capacity and minimize your weaknesses. If you do the math, you'll realize that your time is not cheap, and your work is obviously extremely valuable (Matthew 25:26-27.)

There are a lot of great missionary activities, but as leaders we need to periodically ask this super hard question, and be brutally honest about it: Are we making disciples who obey everything Jesus commanded (Matthew 28:19-20?)

Needing breakthrough on something? In a desperate situation? Don't know where to start? Just asking is a great beginning. It seems that from there God often gives insights into how next to seek and knock. Don't forget to be impudent, though, and especially if it pertains to getting the Bread of Life for a sojourner who desperately needs it (Luke 11:5-10.)

Pray God's Word with your teammates and your disciples (Acts 4:31.) It's a win-win.

Maximize your energy. Professional athletes' work matters little in the heavenly realms, I'm guessing. Yours matters immensely. The quality of their work depends on their energy and strength and health. Yours does, too. Eat healthy food. Exercise a few hours per week. Go to bed at a consistent hour (1 Corinthians 10:31.)

It seems I can always benefit from considering just how many things I want to make my happiness contingent upon. It is wonderful when I can agree with Paul, that to be content all I really need are food and clothing (1 Timothy 6:8.)

Authors and theologians and speakers and pastors are great, but if your goal is to make disciples that make disciples that make disciples, I recommend that you find out who is doing it and do whatever it takes to learn from him/her (2 Timothy 2:2.)

Get ready to use 1 John 1:7 all day, every day. Relationships with teammates and locals are going to be stressed constantly. This verse explains that the fellowship we all long for comes from walking in the Light, consistently clarifying situations with one another. Learn how to 'turn on the lights', sharing your perspective and striving to truly understand others' perspectives as soon as possible.

Don't stop reading at Revelation 7:9-10. You may need this. It's changed my life. When I do not understand, when I am crushed, when I am overwhelmed, when I despair unto life, it helps me to remember that I can trust the One who died for me, and who was predestined to suffer (Revelation 13:8) and submitted to His Father's will.

May God bless you as you pray and obey His Word!
Adam

WEEK 5

Day 33

Coffee break with Keith

Keith Martyn, a British and American dual national, moved to Central Asia 21 years ago in answer to God's call. Keith has spent a total of 15 years in team leadership during his time on the field.

Dear Fellow Leader,

Our Great Shepherd, Jesus Christ, has placed a great trust on you. Jesus has called you to serve Him by faithfully caring for His lambs for whom He shed His precious blood. Those you lead and serve belong to Jesus and caring for their souls, their children, their wellbeing, and their ministries will bring glory to Jesus Himself as He empowers you for this challenging task. As I'm sure you already understand, leadership is not about you but about God, His glory, and His agenda. I pray that, in the words of Henry Blackaby, you will "move God's people on to God's agenda." May I share a few lessons with you from the little I have learned about leadership?

Your ability to lead your team towards Christ and His purposes is based on your relationship with Jesus. As leaders, we tend to be far too busy and it is all too easy to neglect our own walk with Jesus and believe the lie that we can lead God's people in our own strength with worldly wisdom and in spiritual emptiness. Resist the urge to lead in your own strength and embrace Jesus as the leadership solution for every challenge you face. Dig deeper with Jesus each day in the Word and prayer.

Develop a team vision that is so impossible that only God could accomplish it. This will force you and your team into daily humility and faith in God. I like how Bill Hybels describes vision as "a picture of the future that inspires action." Let the faith on the team go wild as you prayerfully paint a picture of the future God has for your team that inspires all of you to action.

Work hard at building trust with everyone. Unity is inextricably linked with God's glory and will be the foundation on which the team can effectively pursue God's agenda. Be transparent with your own struggles. Be approachable. Give of your time and energy. Listen uncritically. Be there for them as though Jesus were as they go through the great times and the hard. Your presence through your teammates' ups and downs will help keep them grounded in Christ and will go a long way towards developing trust and unity.

Believe that God is working in each and every team member and is able to exceed your expectations. The Holy Spirit is at work in each of God's children, convicting them of sin, producing fruit, inspiring them to serve. Be their cheerleader, pointing out what God is doing in and through them.

Communicate constantly. Always be ready to share from the Word and to pray with and for your team members. Communicate the team's vision frequently. Go out of your way to host them. Take time in the middle of your day to call or text them. Check in with them regularly. Seek ways to communicate God's full love, grace, and purposes for them.

Commit yourself to your team members' best even if it means making the painful decision. Not everyone is cut out for cross-cultural ministry. Prayerfully weigh all the input you have about potential team members before inviting them to join the team. You may actually unleash them for greater fruitfulness in God's service if you walk with them in the difficult decision of where they are best suited to serve.

The burdens of leadership are heavy. Jesus calls you to come to Him for rest. His yoke is easy and His burden is light. You are 'yoked in' with the King Himself on this leadership journey. Jesus has much to teach you. Commit yourself to Him in all of your ways and learn from and grow in Him. You will find no better Master than Jesus. Whether you are apprehensive, nonchalant, or a know-it-all about leadership, pray for humility, for God gives grace to the humble but opposes the proud. May God bless you with every spiritual blessing in the heavenly realms in Christ Jesus as you continue on your leadership journey.

May God Bless You!
Keith Martyn

Lunch with Qua

Qua Chocktaw is originally from Pennsylvania, USA, but has spent the last 24 years on the mission field in Southeast Asia, many of those leading a team.

Dear New Team Leader,

Welcome to the field and to your role as a team leader. You are beginning a great adventure. As a team leader, I have had many experiences I never expected. I have moved to a brand new city with very few foreigners. I was with them when my teammates had children on the field. I watched one of my teammates die in front of me, spoke at his funeral, and received his wife and daughter back again on the field as two rather than three. I have been part of exciting times as a team when the first baptisms took place among our focus group and the first house churches were started. I have grieved the departure of teammates who didn't agree with me theologically. Sometimes I have felt deeply understood by my teammates, other times I have felt grossly misunderstood, and – maybe worse – I fear my teammates felt the same of me.

I want to share a few thoughts with you as you begin your role. May this add to all the other great input you are getting from gifted team leaders around the globe.

There are a few things to always keep primary as a field worker and team leader. Serve out of a daily, living relationship with God through continually abiding in Christ and being filled with the Spirit…not out of your ideas, strategies, abilities, or efforts. When you realize this is not the case, stop and take time to re-establish the foundation of your ministry and leadership on the living relationship.

Model obedience to the Word – ministry strategies come and go but the Word endures. Depend on God to work to see your vision accomplished and demonstrate it through prayer, worship and bold trust.

Love your team members, your focus group, your local believing friends, and even yourself; not because anyone deserves such love but because it is God's posture towards us all.

As a new team leader, apart from your personal life, you will have at least seven important roles to play. You will be a learner – a learner of language, culture, community, Church Planting Movement (CPM) ministry, and even the team leader role. You will be an employee; you will likely be involved in pursuing or have direct involvement in some visa-granting activity which takes your time and attention.

You will be a vision-caster. The team, organization, and potential candidates looking at your team are looking to you to see that the team has a purpose, vision, and a plan they are implementing. You are also the person responsible to see that there is evaluation of your progress along the way.

You will be a pastor; the team members, organizational leaders, and sending fellowships are looking to you to see that team members are thriving spiritually, emotionally, and as single/family units.

You will be a CPM worker. Your ability to lead others into CPM ministries will require you to have real, personal experience in finding people of peace, discipleship, mentoring, training, etc.

You will be a supervisor; it is your responsibility to see to that team funds, emergency plans, ministry reports, area leader reports, home assignment reports of team members, team meetings and minutes, and correspondence with candidates for joining your team are properly addressed. (Recommendation: delegate as much and wherever possible.)

You will be a communicator. You are responsible to see that the team's prayer concerns, ministry vision, and regular updates are shared with organizational leadership, sending fellowships, candidates, and partner organizations in a form that keeps momentum and interest in your work strong.

No individual can do all of these well at the same time. Accept that you will have periods of higher involvement in some areas than others and guard against pulling away from field ministry because of the non-field ministry demands. Help your team to see these as team responsibilities and invite their involvement. Know what you do and don't do well and what others do and don't do well and objectively share responsibility among your team members with honest and straightforward accountability among yourselves.

A simple formula that can work well in some cross-cultural ministry teams is the following: Decide things together. Start by determining the purpose of your team as a result of prayer and fasting and studying the Word together. Put this team purpose along with the other core team definitions like vision, values, and expectations for team life down on paper and review them regularly and revise annually as needed.

Formulate the team's written documents, organizational expectations (such as from an international handbook), and the team members' goals into an annual ministry Memorandum Of Understanding (MOU) for each team member to help everyone clearly define what is the responsibility and expectation of each team member. This will serve as a compass for helping your team members advance the team vision in the often confusing and overwhelming context of CPM among an unreached people group. Work with team members to determine and annually evaluate their role and responsibilities in advancing the team's vision and to put that in their MOU. It might sound heavy for some, but the clarity it provides for everyone involved is critical to help people be fruitful in such a changing and undefined environment.

Don't offer input to other team members unless it is either invited or something is happening that is violating the team's purpose, vision, values, and team life practices. Team members will have to cross your path enough, so they welcome the chance to make decisions independent of you.

The collective expectations of your team members are more than you imagine. Expectations shape our understanding of how things should be; thus they must be stated, understood, and agreed upon together. This will result in a set of defined and shared expectations from which your team can operate. Some organizations have a strong facilitative leadership ethos and a decentralized leadership structure. In such circumstances, you will need to work with others' expectations and not dictate them or expect the organization to define them. (I sometimes wonder if the title "Team Facilitator" might better represent the role than "Team Leader.") I have found it helpful to view the ministry team as a group of volunteers offering the time and abilities they bring to advancing a common goal. If you approach your team members as a supervisor over a group of subordinates or a boss over a group of employees, you may be functioning outside the organizational leadership ethos and likely experience conflict in your leadership role.

Generally, we are to help people clarify their roles in advancing the team vision and then help them stay accountable to reaching the goals they have set. The strength of a decentralized leadership focus is its high value of the person and their ultimate accountability to God in carrying out their calling. A weakness is that facilitating the personal expectations and concerns of the team members can have greater influence on what the team does or does not do than the objective advancing of the vision of the team. Facilitative leadership is a sensitive balancing of seeing the vision objectively advanced and bringing along the team members within the potential and limitations of their gifts, family circumstances, and level of adaptation to the cross-cultural context they are living in.

In my team leader role I have learned some people have stronger opinions than they may freely express. Hearing from quieter team members may require drawing them out and helping those who talk freely and frequently to allow others to speak. Invite the help of other teammates or even those outside the team to assist you in helping all your team members being heard and understood.

Don't rush through and yet don't avoid difficult issues. Involve the sending fellowship, your leader(s) and, where appropriate, the team in working through difficult issues with a team member(s). Don't mistake loving others with allowing problems to persist. Seek solutions together and if, in the end it is necessary, make a decision and accept the results of your decision as the team leader. Never attack another's motives or intentions or shame them before others. While you may part ways as team members, make it your goal to be brothers and sisters in Christ who are at peace with each other as a way of honoring Jesus and loving your former team members.

If you remember anything from this letter, return to the first point I shared and what is primary. No team leader has ever been fully capable of carrying out his job by himself. Even Jesus needed the Holy Spirit and the leading of the Father. Make the primary things primary in your ministry; I look forward to hearing someday at some retreat or some conference how God has led you along the journey of being a field leader.

Salam,
Qua

Week 5
Day 34

Coffee break with Blaine

Blaine Hortence, an American, has spent the last 19 years as a missionary to Central Asia. During that time he has spent nine years in leadership including team and field leadership.

Dear Leader,

So, you've accepted an invitation to leadership, have you? I'm sure you've solicited input from trusted advisors, leaders, family and friends. It seems like the Lord is nudging you in this direction, which is great! I do have some advice for you, though. These are lessons that I've learned and realities that I may not have recognized going into my own leadership stints, but which became apparent quickly!

Leadership means dying to self. When you choose to serve others in leadership, there are many 'rights' that you are used to claiming and taking for granted that will now be challenged. Serving others means that you don't always get credit, that you are often inconvenienced, and that you are often misunderstood and second-guessed. It will take time to get used to the feeling. You will need to resist the urge to let people know that they're putting you out, or what a pain they're proving to be. You will begin to understand Jesus' words to His disciples, "How long shall I put up with you?" (Mark 9:19) Nothing's changed, though, except that you've voluntarily signed up for this!

Leadership is watching over souls. To balance the inconvenient dying of leadership, remember the sacred privilege you have of watching over the souls of those under your leadership (Hebrews 13:17.) God has entrusted you with lives for whom He sent Jesus to die.

Be sensitive to the different needs of those you lead. Probably the most startling realization in my leadership was how much time was asked of me from those who are unmarried, especially single women. This seemed to me unfair, at first – their teammates deserved as much time as they did. But then I realized that couples and families had each other to verbally process with, to protect and support them. My leadership was also, to some degree, providing parental protection and spousal insight to single people.

Lead with open hands. The lives of those you lead, the success of their ministry, the goals you set as a team – all of these are, ultimately, in the hands of the Father. Coming to grips with this can free you from inevitable guilt of realizing your own shortcomings and seeming leadership failures. He only requires faithfulness, and only He can measure it.

Enjoy the ride! Serving, growing, learning in community can be one of the most rewarding experiences of your life! We are meant to live in community, and a community committed to nurture church-planting movements is close to God's heart. Yes, you will struggle as a leader and as a team, but always in the shadow of God's goodness and favor. So, why not enjoy it?!

Blessings,
Blaine

Lunch with Daisy

Daisy Lafferty left her home in England nearly eight years ago for South East Asia where she assumed team leadership just two years later.

Dear Friends,

I have been a leader for about 5-1/2 years and, although challenging at times (and many times I have wanted to quit), I can honestly say that overall I love it. I love being able to love and serve people and help them become all that God wants them to be for His Kingdom and glory. I have learned many things along the way (and am still learning!) but here are some of those lessons:

Abide in God. I think this is the single most important thing we can learn as leaders, and it sounds obvious; but the reality all too often is that we get busy and neglect time with God and start working in our own strength. John 15:4 clearly tells us that we can do nothing apart from God; it is only as we abide in the vine that we bear fruit. This includes leadership. It is a task that I believe none of us is capable of and it is only as we abide in Him that we get the wisdom, leading, love, patience, and ability to endure that we need. Ruth Haley Barton, in Strengthening the Soul of Your Leadership, states it so well when writing about God's answer to Moses' concern that people will not follow him. Barton says that people will follow you because you've met with God and because His character is being formed in you. I think another reason to abide is because God is so often more concerned with what He can do in us then what He can do through us, He is more concerned with character then capability. It is only as we abide that God can transform us into Christlikeness.

Know that leaders emerge. I speak particularly here to leaders who are lacking in confidence or do not feel they have all the skills/gifts necessary to be a leader. I spent years feeling (and still do now) that I was not capable as a leader, feeling I didn't have the skills and gifting I needed, comparing myself to other leaders and finding myself so lacking. Then, through the work of Bobby Clinton in The Making of a Leader, I came to understand that we do not start out being perfect, capable leaders, rather we emerge into the leaders that He wants us to be over time. He uses many experiences to shape us, including mistakes we may make. We just need to surrender to the process, allow Him to shape us and do the best we can with His strength and help.

You don't have to do it all yourself. I so often find myself taking on too much responsibility as a leader. I had to learn that I don't have to do it all myself. Firstly, I have a team that can help, and we can delegate some things to them; and secondly we are not expected to be God to our teammates. We are called to love and serve them, but ultimately God is their true Shepherd; and I have seen time and time again God stepping in and doing those things that I could not do.

Invest in relationship. I believe that leadership is relational, so take time with your team, invest in relationships with them, and learn to listen! By 'listen' I mean active listening that pays 100% attention to what they are saying – not only their words, but also what is behind their words. If you are thinking about your response whilst they are talking you are not really listening! One of the biggest problems I have seen in team relationships in misunderstandings. Because of that, listening is so important, as is clarifying what you think they said so that you ensure that what you heard is what they actually said.

Embrace 'multi-cultural-ness'. I have seen that many leaders are fearful of leading people from different cultures, and I do understand the reasons for that. I lead a team of people coming from four different cultures who are serving in a fifth culture, and my experience has been that, yes, it is challenging at times; and certainly the importance of good communication and listening and clarifying becomes even more important across different cultures. However, it is also a beautiful thing, and the benefits far outweigh the negatives. I believe that all cultures reflect God, and it is only as we gather more cultures together that we can be a more complete representation of who God is. People from different cultures bring different things to the team and together we can be more effective for His kingdom – for example, the amazing relational ability of Latin Americans coupled with the strategies of Americans. It also causes us to grow as people as we are challenged by different viewpoints and cultures.

Have a clear team vision. By this I don't just mean a vision statement that states what you are aiming to achieve, but I also mean a vision as to how the team is to operate; set this down in a handbook. When people are interested in joining your team they can read the handbook and see exactly what you are about so that expectations can at least to some degree be aligned, reducing chances for conflict later. Of course, expectations can never be completely laid out at the beginning, but if you have things you want each teammate to do – for example, a home stay for language and culture learning purposes – and you set it out in a handbook, teammates cannot then say, "I didn't know I had to do that," or, "I don't want to do that," because the expectations were laid out at the beginning.

Just because you said it doesn't mean they heard it. A small, and perhaps obvious, thing ...but often I found myself saying something and thinking they heard it only to be frustrated later when they didn't do it or made some mistake because they didn't take on board what I had said. People often need to hear things more than once; this is especially so in their first term where they are taking in so much information.

People often need to learn things for themselves. All we can do is share our thoughts and wisdom with people, and what they do with that is beyond our control. We cannot make them understand or accept what we are saying. Often I find team members coming to me a year later saying they had just learnt something that I had said at the beginning; they had needed to experience it for themselves to learn it. Unfortunately, this means that sometimes they will make mistakes and learn things the hard way. As a leader, this can be frustrating and we can think, "if only they had listened to me…," but that's just the way people often learn.

Lastly, lead by example. We can say a lot to people, but if we are not doing it ourselves how can we expect others to do it? I think that not only are people more inspired and motivated to do things they see people doing rather than merely what they hear people saying, but also our words will have more authority when people see us doing what we are advising them to do.

Well, may God bless you on this journey and may He take you deeper into relationship with Himself as you rely on Him to help you do what He has called you to do, and as you process your successes and failures with Him.

Grace,
Daisy

Day 35

Day of Reflection…

Take a moment to reflect on the 'conversations' of the last 6 days…

- *What portions of the letters did you underline? What struck you or jumped out at you?*

- *Is there anything you disagreed with or would like to have further discussion about?*

- *What themes seem to be standing out to you? How do these things tie together?*

- *Sit for a few minutes and ask the Lord, What would you have me walk away with and take to heart or implement? With whom would you have me discuss this?*

Week Six

Week 6

Day 36

Coffee break with Michael

Michael Edwards, originally from America, began his career in mission 18 years ago. Michael served 10 years in Central Asia, including five years as a team leader before assuming an organizational leadership role.

Dear Leader,

I am convinced that God is at work, at all times, both in me and through me. That is, he is developing me as a whole person – body, mind, and soul; and at the same time, he is seeking to bring blessing to others through me, using my gifts, skills, and the character that he is developing in me. The same is true in my leadership: it is simply a responsibility he gives me, and it is the crucible through which he develops me and blesses others through me.

At a team leader training event many years ago, a speaker shared that "leadership is growing in public." Ouch! I've seen that to be true much too often! As I lead, my failings are right out there for others to see, and my failings in leadership bring pain to those I lead. I would much rather not have those things rest on me.

Yet every time I am tempted to shrink back, I am reminded that leadership is not my choice; it is his call on my life at this point, and he is my Master. I am called to take up my cross daily and follow him. And what I have been blessed to learn is that he is a tender-hearted Master, willing to patiently develop me, wean me from the idols that torment me in their false beauty, and make me into the likeness of his Son – the Son who was crucified in weakness, yet raised in power (2 Corinthians 13:4.)

The great challenge of leadership over time is that we gradually leave our first role – that of being a follower of a crucified Master. The relentless responsibilities we face push us towards a kind of self-sufficient pragmatism; the constant pressure of making decisions without sufficient time and information presses me to find the resources in myself, and my decisions begin to look like spiritualized common sense, rather than the audacious, cross-centered, grace-filled purposes of my Father.

"We always carry around in our body the death of Jesus, so that the life of Jesus may also be revealed in our body" (2 Corinthians 4:10.) I memorized this verse when I was in Bible School, but had no concept of what Paul meant! The process of coming to understand his words has not been a comfortable one, but it has added a richness to my life and leadership that has become bedrock for me. There is no access to the life of Jesus apart from the death of Jesus; but Oh! What life is in him!

So may one of your core commitments as a leader be to daily seek to obey Jesus' call, "Follow me," so that the character of your leadership would flow out of the heart of the gospel, remaining warm and tender as well as bold and courageous!

Blessings,
Michael

Lunch with John

John Robertson has more than a decade of leadership experience, starting in Australia and continuing on to the field in East Asia where he has served for seven years and led a mission team for the last two years.

Dear Leader,

Please do not forsake the work that God is doing within the members of your team. As much as God has a purpose in working through you and them for the salvation of the nations, He has a purpose working in all of you for your own salvation.

Of course it is never our intent to forsake this; it is a statement that we would all affirm. Yet it is one easily forgotten in our life overseas, a new life which is ordered around God's plans for the salvation of the nations, God's plan of salvation for 'them', the unreached, the 'locals', – those who have not yet heard.

We have responded to the call of God, we have set our hearts upon the nations, we have raised partnership and support, we have sold off possessions, we have said tear-filled good byes to those we love – family, friends, churches – we have flown overseas with purpose and intent. It is to the nations we go, to the unreached, to those who have never had a chance to hear the name of Jesus, to receive His grace, to be adopted into his family and made an heir, co-heir with Christ even, of the Kingdom of God. This is why we have left, is it not?

Yet, did we not also leave in order that Jesus might continue His completing work in us? In order that we might be made mature and ready for the return of our Lord?

This is God's gracious, loving commitment to us, and whilst we're on earth, His never-ending work in us. This is what Paul confidently affirms in his letter to the church at Philippi, and James affirms to a broader audience. (Philippians 1:4-6; James 1:2-4) This may not be an ideal message to raise support, but it is an essential way to continue effectively, flourishing for the longer term in the missionary setting.

The setting we move into overseas is like a petri dish. It is an environment perfectly designed to magnify and bring explosive growth in our life. There are the personal stresses… the family stresses… the team stresses… the spiritual attacks …all whilst, for the majority of us perhaps, we're functioning like a social 3-year old as we learn culture and language. Those character flaws we had hidden at home by ignoring certain people and situations that drove us to despair. Those sins that we held at bay through the use of distraction, keeping ourselves busy at work or the myriad options available to us in a culture with which we are comfortable. Suddenly we find ourselves facing all sorts of questions that assault our suitability for the task required.

Am I really 'good enough' for this task? Can God really use a person as broken as me? Maybe I misheard His call? What am I doing here? What made me think I could make a difference? Here I am to 'save' the nations …and I can't even help myself.

This is where an understanding of God's desire to continue and complete His work in you becomes essential. Within this framework these questions are ok; in fact, these questions can be great, for they invite God into the problem. They recognize that He is still doing an important work in us and they recognize that this work will mature us. In having freedom and encouragement to ask the questions, and to invite God into the situation, we begin to discover the pure joy James speaks of, for we know that perseverance will lead to God's finished work in us.

Watch out for these moments. Watch for these opportunities to invite God to come more deeply into the lives of your team members. Look, see, and facilitate the maturing work that God is doing in us all. For their sake, for the sake of your team, for the sake of the ministry, for all of these, yes! But most importantly, for God's sake! This is an enduring desire He has for them and you are uniquely placed to encourage and empower this continuing process.

Dear Leader, please do not forsake the work that God is doing within the members of your team for He has a purpose working in all of you, for your own salvation.

Your Brother,
John

Week 6

Day 37

Coffee break with JFK

J. F. K. Mensah has been in full-time Christian ministry for 36 years. Originally from Ghana, JFK spent four years as a cross-cultural mission team leader before serving as a field leader for another 10 years, and has many years of church leadership experience as well.

Dear New Team Leader,

This is a personal letter to you about some of the things I wish someone had trained or told me before I assumed my team leadership role on the field. Or at least, I wished I had served under a team leader for some time before taking on the assignment. Then came the area leadership of five countries within two years. My past experiences in church leadership faded as I grappled with issues on the field that I had never encountered: language learning as a team, working with the indigenes in our unreached people group, handling administrative issues in a foreign language in a foreign land. As I look back over my four years of team leadership and ten years of area leadership, my wish basket is full.

My team and I arrived full of zeal to work among the indigenes of a particular unreached people group in North Africa and for all the four years we laboured without paying attention to any other tribe or nationality. One team member taught at the university and another was a doctor serving at a clinic and in the community. I trained students in basic computer knowledge. All our labour yielded four national converts from our target people group.

In retrospect, I believe we got some things right. In addition to sending regular newsletters, we prayed an hour every morning and evening, with fasting on Tuesdays and praying halfway through the night on Fridays. Every Sunday afternoon, we gathered interested missionaries in our house to pray for the country and the work. On one occasion, we moved all the evangelical churches in the city to pray in turns for 40 days with fasting. The answers to prayer greatly encouraged us.

Six months before our time of departure, a group of six young men from Togo, Mali, Guinea Conakry, and Algeria approached me to be discipled. They were members of the international church where my family worshipped and I was one of the elders. I was reluctant because it involved teaching the Bible in French, and my French was nowhere near perfect. Moreover, I was unhappy about the time it would take away from my ministry focus.

We started. They came to my house twice or thrice a week depending on my availability. They were hungry for God and His Word. I taught in my broken French. They corrected my French and studied their Bible well. At the end of the six months, I was satisfied with their progress and it was time to go back to Ghana.

Within three years, one of them became the Pioneers team leader in the country. He now serves as an elder in the international church. I could have spent more time on those young men. They knew the country and culture more than my team did. I missed the opportunity of leaving behind me a larger team of well-discipled young men and women.

I got some things wrong as a team leader. Language learning. My team needed to learn French because it was the commercial language. We needed to learn Arabic and the local language of our people group. I was not wise. I led the team to learn all three languages simultaneously. Within six months, they rebelled. It was more than they could bear. It affected our usefulness on the field throughout our stay.

Another challenge was the education of our three children. The English school for them was in another country and not ready for them. We home-schooled for seven months with their books and the children were tired of seeing their parents and Auntie teach them. They wanted to go to a real school. God came to our rescue and answered prayer. All three were admitted, even though it involved school fees that were over the roof and more than 27 trips across the border to send or bring them to school. The teachers were caring and the children forgot us in the excitement of their new environment. Thank God it was a positive experience.

I believe this account is enough to help you in your journey as a new team leader. My prayer is that you will not fall on the same rocks I fell on through improper planning. May God prosper you and give you disciples to carry on the work after your departure.

'Til all have heard,
JFK

Lunch with Tim

Dr Tim Sullivan, an American, has nearly 40 years of leadership experience, including 19 years on the mission field in India and Thailand.

Dear new leader,

I have had the amazing privilege of walking this journey with a huge variety of leaders. Some were very wise leaders, some were high capacity leaders, and some leaders did not necessarily display that they were able to assimilate much from the lessons they had been exposed to. There is a classic old book by Andrew Murray entitled With Christ in the School of Prayer. Clearly the title suggests that Christ has training/teaching opportunities for us, if we would simply join in those with Him. Nowhere is this more crucial than in learning His ways in leadership. There are many things that could be written here. Things to avoid or do differently could easily take the lion's share! However what I've included below are perhaps some of the better nuggets I could give.

First, Proverbs 3:5-6 encourages us to "Trust in the Lord with all your heart and lean not on your own understanding; in all your ways submit to him, and he will make your paths straight." There are a number of things that could be said just from this passage. It provides us with a clear look at one of the great dilemmas of the human heart: we too often trust in ourselves more than in Him, in our own insight more than His wisdom from on high! Bottom line is in trusting Him and relying upon Him to accomplish what He wants to accomplish. Making sure we don't give in to our own understanding of defining what the accomplishment may be. At the end of the day, the thing that He intended to accomplish is often very different from what we thought it was to be.

Second is the importance of how we go about doing this work with others. 2 Corinthians 5:14-17 has much to say to us on this: "For

Christ's love compels us, because we are convinced that one died for all, and therefore all died. And he died for all, that those who live should no longer live for themselves but for him who died for them and was raised again. So from now on we regard no one from a worldly point of view. Though we once regarded Christ in this way, we do so no longer. Therefore, if anyone is in Christ, the new creation has come!" By and large, we could grow in the way we see and treat one another. Do we choose to live as though the way we relate to each other is more important than the actual work we are trying to do? That how we do the work together is as important as the work being done?

The next thing would be not to lose sight of the end goal. Too often it seems that cross-cultural workers get so caught up in the 'ministry' being done and the mechanics of it, that we lose focus on His end goals. Revelation 5:7-9 describes in dramatic detail the price Jesus willingly paid in order to purchase for the Father, as a grace gift, some from every tongue, tribe, nation, and people. While we might be able to find agreement on that reality, we seem to lose sight of what all He accomplished through His death on the cross: He destroyed all of the barriers between humankind and Himself as well as all the barriers within our human relationships. At the same time, He gave to us the message and ministry of reconciliation (2 Corinthians 5:18-20.) Too often, whether in the typical local church or a ministry team, segregation and the dividing walls are allowed to not only exist but they are treated, in the name of greater efficiency, as though they've never really been demolished. It is only as we live in the reality of demolished barriers, by readily crossing them and living without them, that the world can begin to see an unusual, unlikely unity, and be confronted with the manifest power of the risen Christ (John 17.) It is also the way He has decided to display the manifold wisdom of God to all of the heavenly realms (Ephesians 3:10-11.)

Finally, far from the mechanisms and methods of ministry, He has called us to be a fragrant aroma. As we live out reconciled lives in the freedom of dearly loved children, we will in fact be, by His presence being evident in our presence, an aroma. To some, we will remind them of what they are not and do not have, and we will 'smell like death'. But to others we will give them encouragement and hope, and thus we will smell like life (2 Corinthians 2:15-16.) Aside from what we 'do' we simply are/have an aroma. The degree to which we are more alive to His leading and His Spirit's influence, we will be a distinguishing aroma. In 2 Corinthians Paul goes on to make it clear that we are not capable of handling such a weight, but God is the one who makes us competent to be that aroma!

We invest a lot of time and energy getting equipped and prepared academically for ministry. But through the years, it seems to me that it is these 'softer skills' and a character-based relational humility that actually makes the greatest difference. It is an increasing sensitivity to Christ, and His Spirit, and an increased sensitivity and humility toward each other that yields a wisdom from on high and fruit that will last. It is this kind of intimate and intentional growth with Him, and a gracious generosity with each other that provides a sustainability to run the race with perseverance marked out for us. This is not meant to dismiss or ignore the more cognitive, capacity-building endeavors which are needed as well. But the things mentioned above seem to be the really important pearls that are more easily overlooked or lost.

May the Living, Risen Christ grace us to be a people growing more passionately in love with and surrendered to Him, as well as more gracious and humble with each other. May we be marked by an increasing drive to live in the reality of demolished barriers, passionate to see the unique ways His glory is manifest through other cultures. May we be so consumed by Him that we value the sweet nuances of His glory, exalted through every tongue, tribe, people, and nation that He paid so dearly for!

Soli Deo,
Tim

Week 6
Day 38

Coffee break with Stephen

Born and raised in America, Stephan Serkan moved to Turkey 14 years ago as a missionary. Even before departing for the field his role as a mission team leader began, and he has served in various leadership roles ever since.

Dear Emerging Leader,

Greetings in Christ. I was appointed as a team leader before we came to the field and served in that capacity for about ten years. Eight years into the journey I was also appointed as an Area Leader with responsibility for the care of the team leaders with our organization in several countries. I continued to lead a church-planting team for a couple of years before moving to a new city, in part so that I could give more time and energy to my area responsibilities. With that as an introduction I would like to pass on a smattering of things that I have learned through the years.

Prayer is the most important thing you do. Pray on your own. Pray with your spouse. Pray with people of your gender on the team. Pray with the whole team. Prayer is an important part of your care for the people under you. It is essential in church-planting work. If God does not change hearts, we have no hope.

Don't be alone. Find another leader with similar responsibilities and spend time together regularly.

If an issue arises with one of your people, don't wait to talk to your supervisor about it. The longer you wait, the harder it is for your supervisor to give the support you need. Also, don't wait too long to talk to the sending church of your team member. Their involvement in the process is important.

Love people. Whether you have leadership experience or not, whether you think you know the answer or not, people don't care how much you know until they know how much you care. I have made my share of mistakes through the years, but my team members have given me grace because they know I love them.

Leadership is about bearing pain. Don't kid yourself. It's not about power or getting people to do what you want. I'm sure lots of people will tell you that leadership is about serving; and it is. Part of that serving is bearing the pain of those you serve.

There is joy in leadership. As you serve people and they grow and bear fruit there is joy – it's not all hard.

Make sure the team is spending enough time together. We came here with a job to do and if we spend all our time with each other, we won't get anything done; nevertheless, it is important to have at least weekly time together as a team. Building a firm relational foundation now will mean that when problems arise you will be working through them with a strong relational base rather than struggling with building trust and relationship while trying to sort out conflict.

I'm sure there's more, but you'll hear from others and I hope that these thoughts are helpful on your journey.

Grace and peace be with you.
Stephan

Week 6 : Day 38 :

Lunch with Shane

Shane Sparks left Australia eight years ago for Spain where he has served with his wife and children. Four years ago Shane moved into leadership of a team and now a group of teams serving across Northern Spain.

Dear Leader,

I wish that I could write this letter after another few decades of learning and experience. However, I hope that what I have been learning will serve to give you things to consider as you serve in missions team leadership.

Ensure that prayer is central to your life and executing your role. All Christians pray. Even non-believers pray! But there is a vast difference in the people whose prayers are based on an intimate relational connection and those whose prayers are simple business transactions where a prayer is traded for a blessing.

Jesus teaches us that prayer is an intimate conversation with God! He reveals the priority that God's name, Kingdom, and will should have over even our most fundamental and important needs. Since prayer aligns us with God and His activity, the degree to which you constantly and intimately engage with God is the degree to which your leadership and ministry avails itself of God and the transformational power He desires to work in and through you.

So, don't start work before you have related to God personally. In addition to that, I have found it helpful to program intercession for those I lead into my work time. Prioritise prayer and intercession over every other task in your leadership role. Pass time with God, letting Him shape you and then lead you so that you may be the follower that leads others effectively toward Jesus.

The 19th century Scottish pastor Robert Murray M'Cheyne once stated, "My people's greatest need is my own personal holiness." In a world that bases even spiritual leadership on technique, leadership styles, and tools, go to work on your own personal holiness. Together with prayer, your own holiness needs to be one of the highest priorities in your life and leadership.

Perhaps the key to achieving increasing levels of holiness is found in Jesus' charge to His disciples that they must deny their 'self' in order to follow Him. The thing we need to rid ourselves of to follow Jesus is preferring self. Preferring self is as much an enemy to discipleship as it is to leadership. And, of all the enemies to discipleship and holiness, self is the most sinister because it is the hardest to detect and the hardest to remove.

Holiness sets you apart as one who is like God. Since only God can make you like Him, holiness is a relational pursuit of yielding self and trusting God's redemptive work. So pursue Him! And, like Joseph, flee the temptations that seek your attention. Constantly remind yourself that the only source of true and eternal satisfaction is God. Free yourself to grow toward Jesus and far away from the sin that entangles and makes you ineffective and unproductive in your knowledge of our Lord Jesus Christ.

One of the great challenges for new workers, especially from majority Christian cultures, is some belief in the lie that you've come to save the world. This too remains a temptation for leaders. This temptation is just half a step from believing that this role depends on you rather than on God. I believe the main way God disciples us is by putting us in situations that we can't handle alone so that we further learn to depend on Him. Ministry is the obvious and necessary context of this discipleship school, but leadership puts you in the accelerated program! Every challenge of every person you lead becomes a reason to trust God. Obviously, you can't save yourself, but your obedience in fulfilling this role in a godly way will ensure that God continues to save the world through continuing to save you.

The first and main characteristic I look for in new cross-cultural workers or leaders is teachability. It is closely linked to humility and is therefore vital. Further to that, teachability means that the person will grow with others and not always through their own mistakes. Another mission leader has encouraged many of us in leadership development with the principle of prioritising character over competence. Competence will tempt the leader to depend on himself, but a godly character will ensure the leader continues to learn from God and others long-term. Please start asking questions of others, until you become teachable.

One of the big two challenges that I see inherent in the team leader role is the challenge of leading in an organisation that has a very flat or organic structure, like Pioneers. The more hierarchical the organisation, the more organisational authority you have. Organisational authority is not a leadership characteristic, but belongs to management. So a flat structure forces a leader to lead rather than manage. For those of us with experience in management, this transition to leadership is more difficult.

Since leadership is so dependent on influence, relationship is fundamental. Relationship is the medium in which influence flows. I have a phrase written in my office that a mentor of mine once said to me: "Everything moves at the speed of trust." The degree to which you have and create trust in your relationships is the degree to which your leadership will have influence.

The second big challenge that I see inherent to this role is the challenge of leading volunteers. As much as those whom you lead are fully committed in terms of time and effort, they remain volunteers. You do not pay them, you do not offer them any fringe benefits, and often you don't even provide what they need for their work… not practically, relationally, or spiritually. Volunteers add a dimension to leadership that again forces you to lead them rather than manage them.

One of the most important things to remember about being a leader is that there is plenty of grace available from God for all the mistakes you will make. And generally, as an organisation, grace is available in the team context too.

Lastly, please remember that your appointment as a leader is a unique opportunity to grow toward God. If you get that right then you will be fulfilling the majority of your role, and the rest will flow naturally from that posture of dependence on God.

Grace to you,
Shane

WEEK 6

DAY 39

Coffee break with Mark

Mark Singh feels at home in both Singapore and Australia, where he lived prior to answering God's call to mission. Mark served 12 years in India, 11 of those as a team leader.

Dear Team Leader,

One of the key things that is happening within our organisation – and indeed around the world in missions – is the globalisation of the mission workforce. The Lord is even calling people from nations that were previously missionary-receiving nations into His global workforce. We have used the word 'internationalisation' to express the need to become culturally intelligent in the way we do team.

I would like to offer several suggestions to team leaders who will find themselves leading teams that may possibly include Asians, Latin Americans, Africans, and people from other non-Western nations. While this advice is particularly from the Asian context, there are some parallels in other collective, shame-based, non-confrontational cultures. Consider the following thoughts as coming from your non-Western team members:

Please invite us into the discussion. When I am listening quietly in the group, appearing not to be contributing, invite me in by asking me if I have any thoughts to add. Even if I have nothing to say in the meeting, ask me for my thoughts outside the meeting. I probably have something to say.

Please help us to maintain 'face' in the group. Know that I will feel deep shame if confronted, criticised, or questioned publicly. If you need to confront or correct me, please do it gently, on-on-one, and even indirectly (through a trusted mediator).

Please make sure that everything is embedded in relationship. Know that outward harmony is important to me, and maintaining it will be a priority for me.

Please don't assume our silence means we agree with you. Please sometimes ask me what I thought about the matter we discussed as a group, after the meeting. Know that sometimes I may phrase my concerns and what is troubling me in a gentle question rather than a strong statement.

Please ask us if we need help – more than once. I have been trained in my culture to decline help on the first offer – and sometimes even after the second offer. My culture does not encourage me to make my personal needs known.

Please allow longer pauses in our conversation to allow us to jump in to contribute. Hold back so we can jump in to make a contribution.

Please know that we will also adjust to the other cultures in the team. Please allow opportunities for me and other team members from different cultures to explain our cultural norms to each other. It will also help me know how to show you love, respect and concern in your own 'cultural language of love'.

I know that God has brought multi-cultural teams together so that the beauty of all the facets of God's character can be shown amongst us. Multi-cultural teams take more effort, but they are definitely worth it when we start to move in a unity that is borne of the Holy Spirit.

Blessings
Mark

Lunch with Louis

Louis J. Largs moved from America to Central Asia 10 years ago and has been serving as a team leader there for the last seven years.

To Our Replacements,

Our missteps have been many. It has been my sincere hope and prayer that in God's time, we are replaced by those who will improve what we have done here. These are a few things I've learned. You will likely learn many more.

First of all, prepare your heart for the difficult reality that your current vision of God is, in all likelihood, too small and in many ways shaped by the prevailing values of your home culture. Rejoice, though, in the expectation that the limits of that vision are about to be gloriously blown up. Shouldn't this be happening to all Christ-followers in every place? Of course. But what I want to get across to you is that there's something about depending on God cross-culturally that provides a peculiar sharpening to the divine scalpel. Embrace it.

Recognize that, if you're like most of us, you've lost something – or, more likely, never had it in the first place. You are a 'New Testament Christian', a moniker that too often cools convictions about Old Testament revelation. What gets lost? The fear of God. Without a Spirit-birthed fear of God, the Gospel of Christ is only partly understood and partly reveled in – and we will limp along as we minister that Gospel to those who are not just captive to sin, but under the just wrath of an all-seeing holy God from whom no religious system can hide them. Friend, dwell often in the Hebrew Scriptures (the Bible Jesus read, as has been said) and tremble at our God who, before the eyes of His redeemed people, accompanied His presence not with candles and background music, but with thunder and lightning, billows of smoke, the shaking earth, a consuming fire, and sober instructions to fence off the area lest encroachers are struck down. So that you revel more deeply in Christ 'tabernacle-ing' among us, and walk in a manner worthy of His Gospel, drink often of Yahweh in the desert wrapping Himself in the great tent and thick curtains so that the Pure might dwell among those who are not. "Fear God" is, after all, a New Testament command, too.

If you hail from the West, you have been subtly taught (without any ill intent, we hope) that you are an individual soul and accountable to God for yourself. If understood rightly, this is true. However, this can be deceptive and eclipse the more central emphasis in the stream of divine revelation: that each of us is just one in a great and growing gathering. Most of us ignore that the word "you" is predominantly plural in the Bible. Why do I mention this? The universal Church is the Bride of Christ. He gave Himself up for her. Love the Bride. Protect her name and, though her faults are many, be loyal to her and avoid speaking ill of her. Be eager to submit to her – she precedes us by many centuries, and will outlive and outlast us.

Make it your constant prayer that God give you brothers to whom you can entrust yourself – warts and all – and whom you will invite to uncover your blind spots. This world is a spiritual war zone; walking alone is unsafe and unwise. Invite those brothers to often ask what blessing from God is now competing with God in your heart. Is it caffeine or sports or social media or sleep or food or electronic devices? These things are given to enrich our gratitude to God and aid our service for God; we should own them, not them us.

You won't be surprised to hear that enemies will arise during your ministry. There is one enemy, though, that I especially want to warn you about: secret sin. The fall of too many a worker can be traced back to secret sin. You see, there is a strange anonymity in apostolic work: though on one hand you are like the proverbial 'fish in a fishbowl', with local eyes always watching, there is often on the other hand a vulnerable space – a soft spot – between you and the needed protection of your brothers. Strive, with God's help, to hold to a way of life where you always behave as you do in front of those whose good opinion you desire or whose faith you are shaping. You are, after all, ever before the holy eyes of your Father.

You will be often tempted to judge local people by distant standards. If you are from the West, you have been taught that your every opinion is significant and worthy of being aired – the people you serve may believe that wisdom is possessed by the aged and the wise man disciplines his tongue and learns from others. You live by ideals and personal conscience; locals often live by more complicated and troubling realities, and may be ruled by a collective mind. You are expert at wielding resources to avoid inconvenience and pain; they often lack those resources and know pain intimately. Don't trivialize and don't judge …accompany local friends often, but speak only when you must. Pray often and, when you do share, share the divine stories.

Finally, dear friend, become a student of history, and seek out both the writings of departed saints and the companionship of any aged ones who will shun their ailments and give to us who are younger. Be wary of gimmicks and short cuts and silver bullets. That God can do all should not be an excuse for us to do less. That God can overcome our ignorance is not a reason to remain ignorant.

We are thankful to God you are coming. You will never be the same.

His,
Louis

Week 6
Day 40

Coffee break with Hugo

*H*ugo Wolmarans left his native country of South Africa to begin his mission career in Egypt, where he spent six years. He has been the director of Arab World Media for the last 11 years.

Dear New Leader,

Congratulations on your leadership appointment. Leadership is a bittersweet experience – both a blessing, and a challenge – yet also a wonderful way of building up God's people and God's kingdom.

I would like to share with you some of the things that I have learned. I hope they will serve you well as you assume the mantle of team leadership.

To begin with, I wish I had had a much clearer understanding of the expectations of my role before I started. A time of structured overlap with my predecessor and a complete set of files to fall back on would have been a great help!

Secondly, I wish I had had a firmer understanding of the fundamentals of team formation – forming, storming, norming, and performing. How a good team is formed and how it develops into a cohesive unit that performs well together is critical. As Henry Ford said, "Coming together is a beginning, keeping together is progress, and working together is success."

Somebody once asked me, "What are some of the important lessons you have learned as a team leader?" Two things that really stand out for me are the concepts of celebration and forgiveness. These are foundational for any team: the ability to celebrate the small wins — the progress toward vision and strategic objectives — and also the redeeming value of forgiveness when things go wrong, and the ability to say, "Next time it will be better."

In addition to these is the significance of unconditional love for your team members — a love that empowers them to be their best — even if that means they surpass you! Fred Manske Jr said it well, "The ultimate leader is one who is willing to develop people to the point that they eventually surpass him or her in knowledge and ability."

Someone also asked me, "What are some of the mistakes you have made?" My answer would include:

- Appointing people out of desperation to fill a particular role (i.e. the wrong people for the wrong job);
- Intervening too quickly when a project or plan starts going wrong;
- Delaying necessary endings, especially when someone needs to move on. Dragging it out simply prolongs the journey of grief.

Success, for me, is when I see a person taking responsibility, living by God's grace, and being what God wants them to be.

Missionary team leadership is similar to being a team leader in the secular world. However, it is also fundamentally different, especially when it comes to pastoral care, mentoring, coaching, praying together — and doing all these things across cultures.

Grace to you in your journey,
Hugo

Week 6: Day 40:

Lunch with RC

R. C. Stevens left America, following God's lead, for India 15 years ago; a team leader from his arrival, he has also served as a field leader for the last eight years.

Dear New Leader,

Not everyone who calls themselves a leader is actually gifted to be one. The culture of the church has unfortunately held up leadership as a prize (given out rather indiscriminately at times) for those who would volunteer. And so, many in the kingdom today aspire to leadership and find their validation and self-worth in a role they fill instead of a relationship they cherish. It is a sad thing to see someone gifted so obviously in other areas struggle to perform in a role that they should never have been asked to take on in the first place!

Let me make it clear that I believe you are indeed a leader. Gifted by God and confirmed by the community of those around you – people follow you, with or without an official title. And yet I see in you the same struggles of ambition and longing for recognition that I too have wrestled with over the years. You need to know that these longings are normal – most leaders struggle deeply in these areas at various times and with various aspects of pride and jealousy, personal offense, and identity. But you also need to hear that these longings have no place in the Kingdom. They must be put to death, and the only way that can happen is by allowing God to crucify them in you through an unusually painful process of brokenness.

Why am I telling you these things? Because no one ever told them to me. I felt alone in the wrestling of pride and sin and didn't understand the process of brokenness that I now see as so necessary. And I don't want to see you fall by the wayside as so many others have done in the discouragement and brokenness that will come if you want to lead in the Kingdom of God.

So what advice can I give to you? What lessons have I learned the hard way that I could pass on to perhaps spare you some of my pain? Over the years, I've watched many leaders come and go ...wincing at the pain of a new leader like yourself being shaped by criticism and conflict, grieving as others abandon the journey through failure or despair, marveling at the resiliency of those few who have led well and long. I'm sure there are many other things that many others could write much better, so I'll limit myself to a few of the things that have most deeply impacted my own journey over the years.

Don't be impatient. Not all ambition is negative and ungodly. Those who are truly gifted by God to lead will feel the pull and frustration when in situations where the leadership is poor, or as in most cases, simply different from their own. In these situations there is usually a strong bit of naivety as to what leadership truly entails and, at the same time, a fair bit of pride that needs to be dealt with.

Be patient. If God has gifted you for leadership in His Kingdom, He will open the doors in His timing for you to lead. You don't need to push yourself forward. What you do need to do is learn how to follow. If you can't follow someone else, then you will never be qualified to lead someone else. For leadership at its heart is followership – you following your Leader, Jesus, and calling others to join you in the journey. John argues that you can't love someone you've never seen (Jesus) if you don't love those you can see (your brothers and sisters). I'd argue the same thing about leadership. If you can't follow someone you can see, you won't be able to follow the One you can't see. In the end, people may follow you, but you won't be leading them where God would have them go.

Pray more. Out of all the things that I wish I had done differently over the course of my leadership, the one that stands out above all the rest is how little I have prayed. There have been times and seasons where I have prayed much, but they usually have come from desperation and not from discipline. My encouragement would be to build a foundation of prayer – much time spent with God, and more time spent listening than speaking. I have sensed God saying that this is the key to His wisdom and power in my leadership; and yet I still struggle to this day. Pray more than you currently are praying; pray more than you think you have time for; and pray in such a way that you listen to what God has to say.

Truth and Time go hand in hand. I can't tell you how many times over the years I have heard this statement, given as some kind of cold comfort in the midst of a conflict where I have been misunderstood, misjudged, or misrepresented. In the early years of your leadership you will find this advice to be cold and hard – a concrete slab when you want a soft cushion to comfort your soul. We want vindication and we want resolution; but those things usually come after long periods of time, and sometimes they don't come at all. Even so, the statement is true, and in later years you'll find this pithy cliché to be a solid foundation on which to stand when you have to make the hard calls in leadership. God is able to protect your reputation, and what truly matters is what He thinks of you. You must live for the 'audience of one'.

Hit the relationship. When in a time of conflict with someone, or simply a rough patch, keep working on the relational side of things. Our natural inclination with someone who frustrates us or with whom we are having a conflict is to avoid them. Instead, get together informally. Extend yourself more than usual to serve and assist. Find ways to be together outside of the ministry context. I have found that this intentional aspect of working on the relationship can do wonders to help move you through tough spots with those that you lead.

If you have more on your plate than you can do in a day, then you have more on your plate than God wants you to have. It's interesting that God has decreed our day to only be 24 hours – and to have designed us to need about 8 hours of sleep each night. He never slumbers and is working all through the night as we sleep. According to Genesis, God's day seems to start in the evening – "And there was evening and there was morning, the first day…" So we actually wake up in the middle of God's day – He's already up and busy and invites us into His day and His work as we stumble around for some coffee.

The Psalms declare that God gives sleep to those He loves. Ephesians tells us that God has planned in advance for the good works He wants us to do. So what does it say about ourselves when we work ourselves to exhaustion and are always frazzled because we have too much to do? My own guilty conscience tells me that it says I have far too high of an opinion of myself and that I don't really trust God.

But I also think it says something about my laziness. C.S. Lewis talked about how only lazy people were busy, because they won't take on the hard task of disciplining their time and schedule, and so, by default, let everyone else do so! But if God has planned in advance the good works He wants me to do each day, and He also is the one who designed the number of hours and my own limitations in each day, then can I not trust Him to give me just the right amount of things to do in each 24 hours? My guess is that, most often, I don't spend the time listening to God's voice to know which of the things I need to take off my plate and which of the things I need to put on. Why? Because it takes precious time to listen. But if I don't, then I spend much time and energy on things that God isn't interested in me doing that day!

We think that the opposite of laziness is hard work, but what if it really is doing the work that God has us do, and then resting and trusting Him for those things we didn't get to. I have seen so many leaders run themselves into the ground – myself included. I have tried to work harder and smarter. But in the end I found myself simply tired – not more productive, not more strategic. Just tired.

Work hard. But work hard at what God has for you each day. That requires listening. It requires discipline. But it cultivates peace and rest. God is not a taskmaster who lords it over us, His slaves. While we are His servants, He is also our Father and He not only gives us meaningful work, but longs for us to care for ourselves, to have joy and to rest in His ability to 'handle it'. Find a hobby. Keep the Sabbath. And be sure that those you lead see you do these things so that you lead them into health and into rest and into life, even as you work diligently!

When we talk about servant leadership, we are talking about sacrificial leadership. Jesus laid down His life for us, and expects us to do likewise for others. This is especially true when it comes to leadership in the Kingdom of God. And we don't really understand how deep this goes down into our souls until we have to face it on a regular, daily, sometimes hourly, basis. To sacrifice on occasion in a grand way is a grand thing! To every day put yourself last and others first, to count their interests as more important than your own, to continually pour out and have no one seek to pour back in to you …it is draining and discouraging, and a lot like death.

And then Jesus' words come back to us: if you want to be first, you must be last… If you want to have life, you must die daily and take up the cross… In leadership we learn whole new levels of sacrifice, servanthood, and our own sinful resistance to them. And so once again we find we need the cross. We need our flesh to be crucified and our Lord to be lifted up. We need brokenness and humility to be lavishly poured out on our self-satisfied souls. And all of this comes at a cost and with pain. And yet… those who lose their lives truly do find them!

For if God has created you to be a leader in His Kingdom and you choose to follow Him down the path of brokenness, you will find life. God will use you to change lives and futures – and we trust destinies! – of the very peoples we live among.

My hope is that you will find some other leaders around you to journey with. It can be a long and lonely road, and finding a 'band of brothers' to walk it with can make a huge difference. My last bit of encouragement is simply to not give up on the journey and to not despise the pain. The people you lead will at times not seem worth it; but then again, that is the wrong question to ask. We must instead ask if He is worth it… And the answer is "Yes!" every time we ask.

May He be your "yes" every day of your leadership. Know my love and prayers are with you.

Your friend,
R.C. Stevens

Week 6

Day 41

Coffee break with Kaldas

*K*aldas Zaki Masaoud moved from his home in Egypt to serve as a missionary in the Sudan in 1998. In 2002 he became the leader of his team and served in that role until returning to Egypt in 2013.

Dear friend,

As you take your first step in the journey of leading a cross-cultural ministry team, please allow me to offer some tips that I find important to you and to the ministry presently and in the future.

First of all, servant leadership is the most successful leadership style. This means to serve those under your leadership, not that they serve you. Being a leader does not mean you are any better or more experienced than your team members. It means, however, that God chose you to manifest through you how amazingly He can use weak jars of clay to show that this all-surpassing power is from God and not from you.

Use your constant awareness of your weakness, inherent limitation, and insufficient capability to rely on the Lord in whom you can find abundant power and all-encompassing wisdom in every situation. Remember how Moses leaned on the Lord in his weakness (Exodus 2, 3, & 4.)

Remember that your daily relationship with the Word of God (Psalm 119) and your prayer life (Philippians 4: 6) are the pillars for your success. Keep your life holy and always be clothed in white (Ecclesiastes 9: 8.) The fruit of the ministry is dependent on your remaining in Christ, the true vine (John 15; Hosea 14:8.)

Your respect and appreciation of every team member enhances the unity and communal spirit of the team and prevents any sense of inferiority or the formation of factions within the team (Ephesians 4:3.) Your encouragement of the gifts of the team members, even the smallest gifts, is essential for each one to employ and develop their gifts (Ephesians 4:7), bearing in mind that you too had received encouragement from others when you first started ministry.

Remember that for the team members you are a role model. So ask the Lord to help you reflect Jesus in His moral character and daily life (1 Peter 2: 21.) Meet with your team members regularly. Pray together and set your goals and plans over a specified time span, so you can involve them in the evaluation process as well. By so doing you guarantee their full commitment without being mere executers of a vision developed by someone else (Proverbs 29: 18.) This will also ensure continuity even when you are absent.

Bear in mind that transparency and clarity are the shortest ways to avoid problems or solve them if they arise. Take into account that you are not alone in ministry. There are other hundreds, even thousands who faithfully serve the Lord. So be faithful to your role, however small it could be. Yet it is very significant in the Kingdom of God. So neither exaggerate nor belittle your work (2 Samuel 23.) Maintain good relationships with other workers in the country or area, both locals and foreigners. We are all members in one body and we need one another.

Remember that sooner or later you will leave the country. So what would you like the Lord's report about you to look like after you finish and move to a different area, ministry, or even to heaven? The doors open today might be closed tomorrow (John 9: 4-5.) So let us work before the night comes.

First things first: God must have first priority. Secondly comes your family. And then is your ministry. Your spouse and children are more important than your ministry. It is meaningless to succeed as a minister and fail as a spouse or parent (1 Timothy 3: 5.) Trust in the Lord for your children's future and do not worry about them. God will always be faithful and you will experience His compensation.

Do not copy others. But be assured that what the Lord has for you in particular is unique and unparalleled (Ephesians 2: 10.)

Last, but not least, remember that your submission to the Lord and His Word will create a magnificent environment where your team members will subsequently submit to you.

Grace,
Kaldas

Lunch with Flavio

*F*lavio Silva moved from his home country of Brazil to South Asia as a missionary 13 years ago. For the last 10 years he has served in leadership roles including team and area leadership.

Dear friend and harvest co-worker,

I have been asked to share lessons on leadership, and with my own imminent prospect of entering a new phase in ministry – moving on from area leadership – such letter comes in great timing. What could be the most beneficial to share with you? Well, one topic comes to mind.

Over the last decade, I expressed several times the joy that I find in coming alongside of team leaders, and their teams, in their respective journeys. I meant it every time. But I also must say that this joy will be nothing compared to what I will feel on the day I see them crossing the 'finish line'. The day when, like the apostle, they will be able to say, "I have fought the good fight, I have finished the race, I have kept the faith" (2 Timothy 4:7.) So, I intend to share thoughts that will help you not just to continue on the journey, but also to reach its ultimate end in a God-honouring way. Life shows we cannot take finishing well for granted.

You may be familiar with Dr. Robert 'Bobby' Clinton's work. One of the conclusions fleshed out by his outstanding research on the lives of Christian leaders is that only a few finish well. He lists six main reasons behind that, related to: finances, power, pride, sex, family, and plateauing. I will not elaborate on them, but strongly encourage you to read more about Clinton's findings. Instead, I want to write about what I have seen coming before those issues materialise. I want to write about what comes before finishing well.

In my ministry experience, both in South Asia and Brazil, I have confirmed Clinton's findings. But I also noticed that the barriers listed by Clinton represent only the tip of the iceberg causing the tragedies. They are the visible causes, yes; but I am afraid in most cases they are only the 'face' of a 'body' hidden down below. Rarely are these 'icebergs' already formed at the outset; rather they develop along the way in a subtle, dangerous manner. The smaller they are, the easier to deal with them; therefore, the importance of detecting them in their early formation stages. They can sprout and be nurtured from different seeds, but there is one in particular I find worth focusing on. This seed is responsible for most cases I encountered so far.

Over a hundred years ago, Oswald Chambers wrote: "worldliness is not the trap that most endangers us as Christian workers; nor is it sin. The trap we fall into is extravagantly desiring spiritual success; that is, success measured by, and patterned after, the form set by this religious age in which we now live." I have reasons to believe Chambers' warning is more applicable today than ever before. I have seen first-hand this very trap leading too many dear ones towards that dangerous, subtle path mentioned above. As in any heart issue, it is difficult – if not impossible – to detect. Yet, we can watch for external signs. I want to expand on three key areas to keep in mind in order to nurture a desire for spiritual success according to biblical standards.

Salvation history presents abundant examples of how different God's economy may look in people's eyes. In today's world, when visible and measurable results tend to define success, it is crucial for Christ's followers to keep this lesson in mind. Narratives such as the exodus, the disobedience of Saul (1 Samuel 15), Jesus' choice for investing in a few rather than multitudes, teach us how God's perspective contrasts with today's 'normal' values. Concepts like results, growth, task, efficiency, etc. seem secondary, if not irrelevant, in God's plans for His Kingdom. For instance, have you ever thought of how 'inefficient' the exodus was from a human perspective? If we consider that God was prepared to deliver the Promised Land in the first place, one may look at those forty years in the desert as a huge waste of time, resources, lives, etc. But obviously, the God of Israel must operate by very different standards in shaping people after His own heart. In His eyes, unconditional obedience internalised in the heart of His people seems to be far more valuable than any external results (sacrifices). It was by neglecting this value that King Saul was disqualified for the throne (leadership) of Israel (1 Samuel 15.) The same neglect today can be seen in ministry producing fruits that can be seen and measured, but bear no eternal value.

A direct consequence of which economy paradigm we operate under is the locus of meaning. Where do we find meaning? Generally, humans find meaning in success, i.e., accomplishing goals. When success is defined by visible results, people feel meaningful when they are producing those results. Although this works well for the corporate and academic world, not all areas should be bound by these rules. In spiritual ministry, for instance, where hard circumstances abound and ultimately work is invisible, one cannot rely on perceptible results to find meaning. Unconditional obedience demands personal meaning based on faithfulness to the Christian calling. It is not about 'how much' or 'how many', but simply 'how'. In my short field experience, I have already seen too many cross-cultural witnesses developing unhealthy patterns, returning home prematurely or, worse, compromising integrity just to see, or write about, measurable results that can make them feel meaningful. When we are truly connected to the Vine (John 15), all we need is its sap to survive and thrive under the hardest circumstances. Dear friends, the relationship with Jesus is the commodity you cannot live without and at the same time the only one necessary. Find meaning in your connection to the Vine and minister out of it.

Behind the tendency to use visible results to define success and find meaning is the need for control. Ultimately we measure so we can control. It is part of our nature, isn't it? Although we can do that with several processes in life and even with nature to some degree, when it comes to spiritual work we are not in control. In fact, we should not be in control. According to Jesus' words, being connected to the Vine is not only essential for our own spiritual health, but also for the sake of the Kingdom (John 15.) Without this vital connection, much can still be accomplished, but nothing of eternal value. For many, the hardest part of unconditional obedience and Christ-based meaning is to relinquish control. Sometimes, one cannot live without at least the illusion of being in control. Consciously or subconsciously, when we insist in ministering apart from the Lord to keep such illusion, not only do we eliminate the possibility of eternal fruits, but also create disasters that too often end up becoming barriers and stumbling blocks for the very Kingdom we vowed to serve.

We all want to be successful in our ministries, don't we? There is nothing wrong with such desire. In fact, it is a noble one if we let Kingdom standards be our benchmarks. Let the Scriptures set our standards, not the corporate world or the academy. Although we can learn different lessons from these realms, only God's revelation has the power to be efficient in the Spiritual world. Therefore, my dear friends, let's hold the Scriptures close to our hearts as we "run in such a way as to get the prize." Let's all one day have the privilege of finishing well and hear the sweet words from our Lord: "Well done, good and faithful servant" (Matthew 25:21.)

Your servant,
Flavio Silva

Day 42

Day of Reflection…

Take a moment to reflect on the 'conversations' of the last 6 days…

- *What portions of the letters did you underline? What struck you or jumped out at you?*

- *Is there anything you disagreed with or would like to have further discussion about?*

- *What themes seem to be standing out to you? How do these things tie together?*

- *Sit for a few minutes and ask the Lord, What would you have me walk away with and take to heart or implement? With whom would you have me discuss this?*

Leadership Wisdom
Afterword

Mission leadership sometimes reminds me of Buttercup venturing into the Fire Swamp with Westley in the classic film Princess Bride. "We'll never survive," she states rather matter-of-factly. Westley responds, "Nonsense. You're only saying that because no one ever has."

Soon after I became a team leader in an unreached people group, a seasoned missionary mentor commented, "You are engaged in the hardest work in the world." His reference was primarily to the work of church planting. Mentally, though, I added the complexity of leading a team to the mix. I found his words both sobering and exhilarating. If leadership under the best of circumstances is "a great crucible," as one contributor to *Forged on the Field* has observed, imagine the added octane when routine functions of leadership are transposed into a geographically removed, multi-cultural, life- and family-encompassing, spiritual opposition-inciting, multi-stakeholder environment. And yet, despite all the challenges, God's servant experiences a profound joy and a compelling sense of calling and privilege. After all, who else can claim a front row seat in the theatre of God's unfolding redemptive drama?

Amid the tsunami of leadership books in recent decades, very few have addressed the topic of leadership in a cross-cultural mission context, much less in the context of a missionary team. Perhaps readership is too limited? Certainly the sheer interdisciplinary challenge inherent in the topic can prove daunting. Apostolic teams, however, represent the leading edge of Great Commission advance. It's hard to imagine a more critical niche audience.

Maybe it is for these reasons that *Forged on the Field* strikes such a responsive chord. The letters included in this unique volume portray the sun-swept peaks as well as the lonely ravines of leadership. These are 'letters from the trenches', intended for front-line leaders; yet they contain principles and lessons applicable to virtually any Christian leadership context. Flashes of insight and inspiration, blended with vulnerability, encourage those of us who find ourselves embraced in a life and death struggle. Here we meet survivors of the Fire Swamp. We are not alone!

Taking in all of this distilled leadership wisdom, I found myself highlighting a key phrase or sentence in each letter and then composing a list of the Scriptures that have spoken into the lives of these leaders. Themes of endurance, humility, trust, discipline, intentionality, sacrifice, grace, realism, self-awareness and vulnerability began to emerge. One of the challenges of a new leadership role is that many of the most important decisions and precedents will occur early on, when the leader is less experienced. It's a critical time to have a coach or mentor. These letters, taken together, can help illumine the path of any new missionary leader, exposing opportunities and potholes ahead.

Leadership is exhilarating but treacherous terrain. Temptations, trappings, and misapplications of authority can go to the head, narcotic-like. We do well to adopt the posture of the centurion, "I, too, am a man under authority." Faith and submission are inextricably linked. Like Moses, Samuel, David, Daniel, Simeon, and so many others before us, our primary responsibility is to maintain a listening posture before the Lord, and then to respond in obedience. "My food is to do the Father's will," Jesus said (John 4:34.) There is no substitute for the leadership of the Holy Spirit. The best leaders are great followers.

A fundamental axiom of leadership is that it always plays out in a context. "When David had served God's purpose in his own generation, he fell asleep" (Acts 13:36; see also Psalm 138:8.) Leadership is made easier when the context of one's own contribution is more fully understood and accepted. In our case, context includes theological, cultural, missiological, sociological, organizational, generational, and personal dimensions – to mention just a few facets of the leadership diamond. A helpful exercise may be to trace such themes through this volume. In short, always keep your role in perspective, relative to the bigger picture.

Church planters, team leaders, area leaders, etc., all serve in complementary capacities. One might imagine leaders functioning at different 'altitudes', just like aircraft or birds or insects. An eagle may soar majestically overhead, but it can't hold a candle to the sheer aerodynamic maneuverability of the common housefly. All kinds of leaders are needed. You will do well to ascertain your optimum altitude for the role God has given you, while being supported and informed by those with differing vantage points.

As a team leader, you will want to keep in mind the needs and realities at the grass roots as well as the higher missiological and strategic altitudes – always without losing focus on your own unique contribution. Your task as a team leader is to build and serve your team, helping them to pursue God's will together over an extended period of time. While you may prefer to invest yourself in specific grass-roots ministries as in the past, you may need to sacrifice some of these (preferably not all) in order to achieve an even greater good through the combined efforts of a growing and maturing team.

'Context' includes the liberating recognition that you and your team are making a modest but significant contribution, during a certain period of history, in a particular culture, as part of the larger body of Christ. Some have likely gone before you, and others almost certainly will follow. As a pioneering team, it is quite likely that your role will be to do the "hard work" (John 4:38) of laying a solid church planting foundation on which others will build. Pray to see a significant harvest during the lifetime of your own ministry. If you don't, do not yield to discouragement. As you daily submit to the Lord of the Harvest, you can rest in the confidence that you are effectively running your leg in the redemptive relay. Your team may be called to till and sow, to "chuck rocks," as one recent friend and martyr put it, so that others may someday reap. Sow your seed with diligence, faith, and skill.

Leadership is generally a marathon, not a sprint. You may grow frustrated as you serve through others, surmising that you could perhaps do a better job yourself, at least in some areas. Or you may grow discouraged as team members, in whom you have invested, grow disillusioned or even abandon ship. Your job is to keep your sights on the bigger goals of walking with God, communicating the gospel and strengthening believers according to the Scriptures. Ultimately you cannot set goals for others or guarantee a particular outcome. As we wholeheartedly follow Christ we hope, trust and pray that others will be influenced toward his purposes.

Management gurus Drucker, Covey, and Bennis frequently remind us to "begin with the end in mind." A central part of your role and responsibility is to continually articulate a clear picture of the end goal as well as the envisioned path toward achieving it. This will require leading the team in a continual process, year after year, of collaborative rediscovery and realignment. This ongoing cycle involves frequent interplay between vision (the 'what/where'), philosophy of ministry ('why'), strategy ('how/when'), and the interpersonal dimension ('who'). It's tempting, but rarely helpful, to find short cuts around this thoughtful process. Unless one has an architectural design in hand, many mistakes will be made in the construction of a building. Some team leaders, unfortunately, are weak in this area of envisioning the end goal and then gently but persistently coaching the group toward the shared vision.

A final thought with regard to your leadership legacy: Through the years I have found it helpful to ask, "How am I investing in the five key areas – by way of prayer, people, institutions, ideas and tools?" What are your main burdens in prayer? Can you name the individuals you are currently sponsoring, mentoring and developing? Remember, leadership is more caught that taught. Institutions include such human 'organisms' as your team, the local church, a training program, or the agency in which you serve – all of which can develop an enduring life and impact of their own when properly nurtured. What ideas are important to you? Do others view you as an expert in a particular field of endeavor, or a passionate proponent of an important concept? Finally, are you producing specific tools that others will be able to wield for God's glory? You may find that you yourself, and other members of your team, are especially gifted in one or more of these areas.

Has *Forged on the Field* whetted your appetite to go further and deeper in your leadership journey? Would you value an opportunity to share the journey with your counterparts around the world? We welcome your participation in a growing leadership community by joining the dialogue at: www.peregrinipress.com/Forged.

"And David shepherded them with integrity of heart; with skillful hands he led them." – Psalm 78:72

May the Lord of the Harvest strengthen your heart and hands for the work ahead.

Steve Richardson
President
Pioneers USA

FIELD NOTES SERIES OVERVIEW

BOOK 1
FORGED ON THE FIELD
LETTERS FROM GLOBAL MISSION LEADERS

BOOK 2
VOICES OF THE FIELD
ADVICE FOR PROSPECTIVE MISSION WORKERS

BOOK 3
PREPARING FOR THE FIELD
PERSPECTIVES ON PREPARATION FROM SUPPORTERS, CHURCHES, AGENCIES AND TEAMMATES

BOOK 4
RETURNING FROM THE FIELD
FINISHING WELL, LEAVING THE FIELD AND RETURNING TO THE HOME CULTURE

Made in the USA
Charleston, SC
29 September 2015